T0345545

THE CRIME OF JEAN GENET

THE FRENCH LIST

RECENT TITLES FROM THE FRENCH LIST

ROLAND BARTHES
Essays and Interviews
Volume 1: 'A Very Fine Gift' and Other Writings on Theory
Volume 2: 'The Scandal of Marxism' and Other Writings on Politics
Volume 3: 'Masculine, Feminine, Neuter' and Other Writings on Literature
Volume 4: Signs and Images. Writings on Art, Cinema and Photography
Volume 5: 'Simply a Particular Contemporary'. Interviews, 1970–79

RENÉ CHAR
'The Inventors' and Other Poems
Hypnos: Notes from the French Resistance, 1944–45

FRANÇOIS JULLIEN
This Strange Idea of the Beautiful
The Philosophy of Living

YVES BONNEFOY
The Anchor's Long Chain
Rue Traversière

PASCAL QUIGNARD
Abysses
The Sexual Night

ANTONIN ARTAUD
50 Drawings to Murder Magic

HÉLÈNE CIXOUS
Tomb(e)

GEORGES PERROS
Paper Collage

Dominique Eddé

THE CRIME OF JEAN GENET

Translated by Andrew Rubens and Ros Schwartz

LONDON NEW YORK CALCUTTA

PAP
TAGORE

The work is published with the support of the
Publication Assistance Programmes of the Institut français

Seagull Books, 2016

Originally published in French as *Le crime de Jean Genet*

© Éditions du Seuil, Paris, 2007

First published in English translation by Seagull Books, 2016

English translation © Andrew Rubens and Ros Schwartz, 2016

ISBN 978 0 85742 339 9

British Library Cataloguing-in-Publication Data
A catalogue record for this book is available from the British Library.

Typeset in Dante MT Regular by Seagull Books, Calcutta, India
Printed and bound by Maple Press, York, Pennsylvania, USA

To J-M D

He gave me the feeling of a frozen fire. His gestures were as calculated, precise and full of meaning as his words. He would switch from action to stillness in such a composed, agile way that still today the two overlay each other in my memory. I can see his hand, raised slightly—the Gitane held shakily between his index and middle fingers, smoke floating over his long, tobacco-stained nails—I see it glide, barely moving, without the slightest tremor as it brings the cigarette to his lips, then either returning to its weightless state or settling on a knee to sleep there, like moss on a stone. There was such a mixture of authority and passivity, lethargy and resolve that it was impossible to relax while looking at him. Everything was so controlled, so slow on the one hand, so rapid on the other. Never a sudden start, nor any sudden braking. But always vigilant, ready to fire. Genet's movements mimicked the movement of time accumulating rather than passing. This created a sort of closed, musty atmosphere which evoked the marriage of a death and a rose. His two favourite flowers.

The shadow on his face, all the shadow, was concentrated in one place, beneath his eyebrows. His eyes with their almost lashless lids were two little pools of blue. A blue flecked with white and bronze. His intense, direct gaze came from so far away that it had no surface. Unyielding. Hot and cold. Good and evil. Free to do anything, including to turn his back on someone facing him. In his gaze Genet had the same capacity for slowness—for emphatic hesitation—as in his speech. It was never a sign of weakness, it was his wild side—he prowled round the territory before pouncing. It was also his love of theatre: the pleasure of toying with the curiosity or fear he aroused. Lulls amused him. But they were more than that. Silence, for him, was an opportunity to apply pressure and to create. His power and presence intensified when he fell silent. During those moments, his eyes took over from his voice, fixing upon his interlocutor or on a particular point in space, and holding the phrase in the way a note is held and extended on a piano. As for his sadness, no matter how he tried to cloak it, to convert it into the most neutral gravitas, it would still rise to the surface, even in his infallible malice. Then his gaze was unquestionably at its most powerful; the combination of the two was its essence.

There were no colours in his voice, or, rather, there was only one. Its sound was short, electric, metallic. It was not a resonant voice, but all the same, it was captivating. I can still hear it, half-playful, half-witch, with a screeching caused by the friction between the child and the monster. He enunciated and punctuated intensively, rattling out the syllables, presenting the phrase fully formed, like a diktat, delivered with amused vengeance. Nothing he said—neither the dazzling nor the outrageous remarks—was the result of chance or inadvertence. He pulled apart the absurd in the same way as reality. Or, rather, for the absurd to have *meaning* in his eyes, it had to be the result of a trap, a farce, a set-up—ideally of his own devising. He had no interest in the inconceivable. He mastered speech and silence to an equal degree, drawing on both to make himself heard. He gave little performances. Formidable mixtures of irony and precision, of calm and impudence. He was not intoxicated by the speed of his thoughts, but he savoured without turning a hair the bewilderment of his interlocutor. He took hold of his listener, he took control. And he who hated orders forced himself into an absolute, impenetrable, all-powerful solitude in order to issue his own. He was, in a sense, the anti-terrorist of our age. He did not call God as his witness but as his enemy, fighting him, setting himself against him, dreaming of seeing him die. Because, before being men, were not his enemies—whites, the rich, the custodians of society—first and foremost the vile progeny of God the Father? They who would never know the enviable tragedy of shame transformed into a bastard's pride. Catholicism is everywhere in his work. It is the central motif, without which the whole canvas would disintegrate. Its vestments, rites, angels and archangels, its bells, censers, tabernacles and its Jesuses—Genet robbed the Church and its ornaments in order to commit his parricide. He created and exalted a new god out of the ashes of the first: the murderous lover, the orphan Christ, sentenced to death and crowned with 'rose thorns'.[1]

God—the word god—was only used by Genet if he was ridiculing it or undermining its meaning. He was constantly luring it over to his side, acclaiming it, beguiling it, paganizing it, making it into 'a sky which is not a ceiling'.[2] His God carried ballast. He could play with him, kill him slowly, then revive him, blowing on the embers. However, he could only overcome and kill his father—who, unlike God, had the misfortune of actually existing—by denying him utterly. By erasing him. God is the only father to be found in Genet's works. There is not the shadow of any other father, anywhere. Neither in his novels nor in his plays. There is no more a genitor to be found than there is solid ground beneath the foot of a tightrope-walker. This strict absence, which critics, surprisingly, have not picked up on, is forever coupled with a transfer which is both abstract and relentless. Driven out, the father finds his place beyond the 'ego', outside. He has become order, the state, society, the world's police. The West. The power of

1 See Jean Genet's poem 'The Man Condemned to Death' (1942). English translation by Mark Spitzer available at: http://goo.gl/kVH8qU (last accessed on 28 October 2015).

2 See Jean Genet, *Miracle of the Rose* (Anthony Blond trans.) (New York: Grove Press, 1988), p. 43.

the whites. Colonizers. The law. Let us recall incidentally that when Genet, at seven months old, was entrusted to the care of the state, it was written down in black and white that from then on the state would hold 'full rights of paternal authority' over him. The adolescent Jean Genet retaliated against this fate through a very simple equation, with immeasurable consequences: he decided that 'lawless' = 'fatherless', with no exceptions. Better: in a role reversal of utter audacity, he decided that as it came to one against all, if he was freed from the superego, *he* would be the superego.

And when one of his characters dared to break this rule, this is how he would go about shutting him up:

VILLAGE. My father once told me . . .

ARCHIBALD (*interrupting him*). Your father? Sir, don't use that word again! There was a shade of tenderness in your voice as you uttered it.

VILLAGE. And what do you suggest I call the male who knocked up the negress who gave birth to me?

ARCHIBALD. Dammit, do the best you can. Invent—if not words, then phrases that cut you off rather than bind you . . .

VILLAGE. What can I substitute for the word father?

ARCHIBALD. Your circumlocution is quite satisfactory.[3]

---

3 Jean Genet, *The Blacks: A Clown Show* (Bernard Frechtman trans.) (New York: Grove Press, 1988), p. 26.

All of his characters—louts, sailors, pimps, murderers, convicts, whites, blacks or Arabs, militiamen or *légionnaires*,
soldiers or judges—were, without exception, only ever the
sons of their mothers. And even then, only here and there,
because these women turn up very rarely, they are barely
even mentioned. They appear fleetingly and are downtrod-
den when not hysterics or madams. Most of the time they
are maids. Like Eugénie Régnier, Genet's foster mother,
was before her marriage and, above all, like Camille Genet,
his birth mother, about whom we know almost nothing
other than that she was unmarried and a *femme de chambre*.
In fact, it is possible that the continuous inversion of the
roles of the two sisters in *The Maids* (1946) is in part a result
of the tension, indeed the extreme psychological difficulty,
that Genet experienced when writing characters so closely
associated with his secret self. Solange and Claire move
towards crime with hesitant, contradictory, incomplete
steps. They never stop shedding their skins; they almost
never are who they are. Genet sends them from one per-
sona to another with the skill and urgency of a juggler with
balls of fire in his hands. When the spectre of his mother
drew too near, he found himself forced to thwart it, warding
off the danger of the ghost's appearance by distorting the
features of the maids, making them into 'Madame'. Perhaps it is also this—the risk of losing control—that led him
to depart so far from the real crime that provided the play's
inspiration: that of the Papin sisters, Christine and Léa, the

two maids who, following a violent incident inflicted on them by their mistresses—a mother and daughter—killed them both, hacked them to pieces and gouged out their eyes. It is probably also no coincidence that the little orphan maid in *Funeral Rites* (1947), the mourning lover of Jean Decarnin, is the only character who escapes utter sordidness. The honour of closing the novel falls to her, a daisy in her hand, in a patch of moonlight. An honour which she owes, it must be said, to the perfection of her misfortune. For if she had held on to her man, or even his child, which she had carried, Genet, her saviour, would not have spared her.

To be granted, from his pen, the status of a real mother, a woman had to be Arab or black. Only three women attained this favour in his work: Saïd's mother in *The Screens* (1961), Félicité in *The Blacks* (1955) and above all Hamza's mother in *Prisoner of Love* (1986).

All in all, Genet's only creator is himself. It is his creations who re-create him, multiply him, perpetuate him and drive him; it is they who offer him up the 'crime' which, he feels, left him an orphan. There is not a crack between him and them, not the shadow of anyone else. They light up or disappear at the touch of his finger like the lights in a theatre. Unlike most of literature's great fictional characters, whose lives leave their authors behind like birds flying the nest, his are nothing without him. Antigone, Hamlet,

Emma Bovary, Le Père Goriot, Raskolnikov, Swann or Charlus, Nostromo, Quentin and Bloom became part of the world once they were brought to life. Even the characters of Kafka and Beckett, who belong nowhere, stopped belonging to their authors. With Genet, the cord is never cut. Whether they are named Mignon, Bulkaen, Divers, Querelle, Harcamone or Notre-Dame, Genet's monsters, heroes and 'beautiful murderers' have no past or future, they are written with the foreknowledge of the corpse that awaits them. 'It is my way of possessing those I love,' he wrote to Cocteau. 'I wall them up alive in a palace of words.' Cursed offspring, cut off from the world, at the first stroke of his pen they become children of the purest, most intense present, in which 'eternity flows in the contours of a gesture'.[4] This is how Genet succeeded in capturing the execrable and the sublime within the same fabric, without the stitches unravelling. He constructed his phrases in the manner of dreams, in a motionless progression; pushed into a time beyond time where breathing battles the scarcity of the air, beauty and death their own estimation of each other and poetry the licence to kill.

When did I meet Jean Genet? It is hard to remember the exact date. What I am sure of is that I met him through Tahar Ben Jelloun, at the start of the war in Lebanon. It must have been in 1975. I would have been twenty-two, and

4 Genet, *Miracle of the Rose* [our translation].

he sixty-five. Fascination is not a word I like, but I can think of no other that better captures the feeling he inspired in me. He fascinated and intimidated me all the more in treating me—like all those to whom he provisionally opened his door—as an equal. It was generosity, but it was also something else. Genet composed situations as though they were books, or paintings. He seemed to wield the same influence over people as he did over words. He would try to draw out something different to what they were, something more. In my case, his intelligence gave me wings—and clipped them. I was both enthralled and uneasy in his presence. This may seem like an impossible combination, but it was the case. Of course, while he played a not insignificant part in my life, I was, on the other hand, a latecomer of only secondary importance in his. At the time I knew him, though far from having read all of his work, I had sampled enough to know that under the alluring titles of *Miracle of the Rose* (1946) and *Our Lady of the Flowers* (1942), the scent of fate mingled with the stink of latrines. Transfigured by the beauty of his language, his perversion reached heights which simultaneously oppressed and exalted me. My perception of the connection between the writer and the man remained hazy. I believe this was the case for many Arabs. Let us say, speaking only for myself, that I was under the influence—but I was also learning about freedom.

'Since you love writing,' Genet once said to me, 'read the greats, read Victor Hugo[5] and Chateaubriand, *Things Seen* and *The Genius of Christianity*. Read Nerval's poetry as well.'

I wondered for a long time why Genet, unlike Céline, had adopted the language of his 'enemies' rather than inventing one that resisted it. Why had he chosen his 'gods' in the heavens he dreamt of tearing down? If we connect the word god with the—unutterable—word father, the answer seems simple, at first glance. Since his maker, that bandit of a progenitor, left no trace of himself, apart from the dazzling success of a spermatozoon, the son had to borrow a template in order to have an image of him to strike down. And the template needed to be both hostile and grandiose. The combination of Christianity and Romanticism suited perfectly. By magnifying the image, Genet found the means both to build it up and to reduce it to nothing. Better, he found the means to strike right at the heart of Romanticism, to capture its movement as one bridles a horse, and—holding its syntax sacred but emptying it of its life—to gather up its ghosts at the centre of a world that was answerable to him and to him alone.

---

5 In 1969, writing to Antoine Bourseiller, Genet said that Victor Hugo was 'a talented man, bereft of the tiniest scrap of genius'. When he spoke to me, 10 years later, of the 'genius' of *Things Seen*, I could not help thinking of the similarity of titles like *Notre-Dame de Paris* and *Notre-Dame-des-Fleurs* or *The Last Day of a Condemned Man* and *The Man Condemned to Death*.

But how did he go about admitting to himself that his adulation of crime and murderers would only come into being through classical forms of beauty—I almost wrote 'classy forms'—a beauty inescapably destined for readers unlikely to be former convicts or future lovers?

> It was necessary for me to address the enemy precisely in his own language . . . If I was seduced by language—and I was—it wasn't in school; it was around the age of fifteen, at Mettray, when someone, probably by chance, gave me Ronsard's sonnets. And I was utterly dazzled. I had to make myself heard by Ronsard. Ronsard would never have tolerated slang.[6]

This is the essence of Genet, with humour and seriousness inseparably interwoven. Making war on France while making love to its language was his way of humiliating the country twice: bringing it to its knees, and cuckolding it. But 'to make himself heard by Ronsard' . . . wasn't that something else?

'The reader, reading him, actually becomes Genet,' wrote Sartre. I do not think that the author of *Saint Genet* (1952) was right on this point. In fact I think the opposite is true. If there is a body of work in which it seems to me that the

---

6 Jean Genet, *The Declared Enemy: Texts and Interviews* (Albert Dichy ed., Jeff Fort trans.) (Stanford, CA: Stanford University Press, 2004), p. 196 [translation modified].

reader is deprived of identification—deprived in the religious or penal sense of the word—it is surely his. Not because we find Genet's sadism and masochism exclusory, but because his manipulation of them exerts itself and flourishes at our expense, against us—and often (need we be reminded?) against our most fundamental notions of morality. Our place, you might say, is decided upon, pinpointed and designated by him in advance. And for those of us—those of 'you'—who chose to ignore this, strong reminders appear everywhere. 'Please take into consideration that I am seeking to define a moral attitude and to justify it,' he wrote in 'The Criminal Child' (1949).[7] 'I admit that I wish above all to perform it, and in doing so to oppose you.'[8] This 'you', which Genet uses abundantly in his writing, is never a sign of reconciliation. It has a menacing undertone; he brings it out each time his distance from the reader is threatened, each time there is a chance of the latter being overcome by the desire to understand, or worse, by empathy. Genet definitely wanted to be feared, admired and loved, but understood? On no account. When, on one occasion I was talking to him, I naively confided that I had 'discovered something', he replied, without batting an eyelid, 'I am not America and you are not

---

7 Written in 1949, 'L'Enfant criminel' (The Criminal Child) was commissioned by RTF (French radio) but was not broadcast due to its controversial nature. It was published in a limited edition in 1949 and later integrated into Volume 5 of *Oeuvres complètes*.

8 Genet, 'The Criminal Child' [our translation].

Christopher Columbus.' If he had known that, back from America, I would one day decide to write a book . . .

But who knows? Perhaps things are not so simple. It could be that in urging me to read *The Genius of Christianity* (1802), Genet really did intend me to discover the very paths I found. For example, the extract from Milton's poem, quoted by Chateaubriand, in which the devil speaks: 'Farewell happy fields, where joy forever dwells: Hail, horrors.' And these lines from the end of his speech:

> But say I could repent and could obtain
> By Act of Grace my former state; how soon
> Would highth recal high thoughts, how soon
>   unsay
> What feign'd submission swore? . . .
> This knows my punisher; therefore as far
> From granting he, as I from begging peace . . .
> So farewell Hope, and with Hope farewell Fear,
> Farewell Remorse: all Good to me is lost;
> Evil be thou my Good.[9]

What other author turned these parting words of the devil into their own creed with more fervour or obstinacy than Genet? One can imagine the half-fascinated, half-derisive look in his eye as he read over Chateaubriand's annotations. Especially as he read this one:

9 John Milton, *Paradise Lost* (1667), BK 4, lines 93–6, 103–4, 109–10.

When, with the greatness of the subject, the beauty of the poetry and the natural majesty of the characters, such a deep knowledge of the passions is displayed, we can ask nothing more of genius . . . Satan taking charge of the dominion of evil for all eternity: this must, if we are not mistaken, be one of the most sublime and pathetic conceptions ever to have come out of the mind of a poet.[10]

In merging their roles, Genet did better than Milton and worse than Satan: he single-handedly assumed the evil and the beauty which respectively horrified and enchanted the great champion of Christianity. He completed—perfected—his work of parricide. With this approach, using regal language to demolish all boundaries between fantasy and reality, he turned the weapons of his symbolic fathers against them. Against the great poets of the French language, who had been, moreover—at least in the cases of Nerval and Chateaubriand—famous orientalists as well. As for the portrait the author of *Memoirs from Beyond the Grave* (1849–50) painted of the demon of pride—the serpent—I saw, as in a dream, Genet's amused smile floating above it. He was charmed by the writing like the animal charmed by the shepherd's flute, and seemed to find himself reflected in its mirror:

10 François René-Chateaubriand, *The Genius of Christianity; or, the Spirit and Beauty of the Christian Religion* (Charles I. White trans.) (Baltimore, MD: John Murray, 1856), p. 112.

This incomprehensible reptile . . . like a light azure vapour, or the gleams of a sabre in the dark . . . An object of horror or adoration, they either view him with an implacable hatred, or bow down before his genius. Falsehood appeals to him, prudence calls him to her aid, envy bears him in her bosom, and eloquence on her wand. His colours . . . possess the false splendour and deceitful variety of the seducer.[11]

A century later, the author of *Miracle of the Rose* wrote: 'I cannot but think that seduction is only possible when one is not quite oneself.'

From Cocteau and Sartre, who praised him to the skies—to the point, in the latter's case, of endangering his own choices and principles—to those who today furiously set themselves to hunting down the tiger or the serpent with a butterfly net, there are misinterpretations everywhere. This is exactly what Genet wanted. The little nuggets he knowingly and meticulously sowed are more often land-mines than clues. Neither our earnest mine-sweeping nor our ambition of pinning down, once and for all, that he was this or that have any sense. He was both, this *and* that, and possessed of a fierce capacity to—impassively—send either up in smoke. This was his freedom. 'If I take contempt with a smile or a burst of laughter,' he wrote, 'it is

11 Ibid.

not yet—and will it someday be?—out of contempt for contempt, but rather in order not to be ridiculous, not to be debased, by anything or anyone, that I have placed myself lower than dirt.'[12]

Those who seek to 'understand' this are better off rereading Dostoevsky rather than sullying themselves playing at being a lawyer or moral crusader. To limit oneself to just one of the two Genets is not only to get bogged down in insoluble digressions—it is to let oneself be taken hostage, by him and by oneself. For this prison recreated in his works, a prison worthy of his dreams, it was not enough for him to merely revel among his own kind, the murderous children. He went as far as to lock up his reader too, and wildly enjoyed his role as jailer, watching the reader struggle, attracted by his words like an insect towards the light, torn between unease and admiration.

If he invented us, as he invented his settings and his language, it is up to us to steal from him in return. Rather than playing at arbiters of good and evil, we need to break out: climb a watchtower and see the great man's shadow shrink down to human size. Everyone, he said, 'takes on their true dimensions once they are dead. This, I think, is the meaning of Mallarmé's line "eternity at last made him into himself".'[13]

---

12 Jean Genet, *Our Lady of the Flowers* (Bernard Frechtman trans.) (New York: Grove Press, 1991), p. 116.

13 From Stephane Mallarmé, 'The Tomb of Edgar Poe' (1899) [our translation]. Peter Manson's English translation of the poem is available at: http://goo.gl/sVHGGM (last accessed on 29 October 2015).

It was shortly after the massacres of Sabra and Shatila, at the end of 1982 and beginning of 1983, that Genet turned his back on me, or, to be precise, sent me packing. There were three of us in a restaurant on the rue du Bac: Leïla Shahid, Genet and I. The scene he improvised that day should not have surprised me. He was true to himself and did what he had always done: betrayed and broke off without compunction. There was something quite slapdash about it, his first (and last) attack on me. The pretext was crude, as was the lie. But I say to myself, as I think of it again, that, in a sense, he spared me. That, in his case, handling me with kid gloves would have been real crudeness.

Constantin Tacou, the director of the publishing house L'Herne at the time, had asked me to relay his wish to devote a book to Genet—one of their famous *cahiers*. I hardly knew Tacou. We were neighbours on the rue de Verneuil. Cioran had introduced us a few years earlier. I had immediately responded to the request by saying that I strongly doubted it would be well received, but that I would 'pass on the message if the opportunity arose'. Which is exactly what I did, over that ill-fated meal. 'Why didn't you ask him to do a *cahier de L'Herne* on the Palestinians?' Genet immediately retorted. 'Do you seriously think there would be any chance of that interesting him?' I replied, without foreseeing the blow that was about to follow. 'And what about you?' he added, icily, 'Why haven't you written anything about the massacres? Why?' I was dumbfounded. Genet drove the nail home: 'It's because you don't care. That's why. It's because you don't care about the Palestinians. What interests you is the *cahiers de L'Herne*, Parisian publishers and *Libération* . . .' I tried to defend myself, to reason with him, to counter him. Which was stupid: his decision to have done with me had been taken long before this grotesque accusation. I was surprised, shortly after, at how little resentment I felt. I was barely angry with him. From which I today conclude that, to a certain extent, it suited me not to see him any more.

It is at this moment—as I write and read over these words—the likely reason for Genet mentioning *Libération* in his diatribe comes to me: on the day of Sartre's death in March 1980—I was then working for Éditions du Seuil—a journalist from the paper had phoned me to ask if I would request a testimony from Jean Genet. The latter, when I explained my reason for calling, snapped back, 'Tell them that a puff of smoke has gone.' I refrained from communicating his response.

I had the feeling, and I have it still, that this wisecrack, fired like a bullet from a gun, was aimed in several directions at once; that it was also directed towards the part of him that resisted his supreme indifference. Genet treated his sorrows as parasites, he killed them. No one, not even he himself, could tell which of his two selves had the upper hand, deep down. We had talked of his relationship with Sartre, a while before. 'He had a lot of humour,' he had told me, 'people forget that.' He had concluded, as if talking to himself, 'We shared a lot of laughs together.'

On one of the last occasions we saw each other, in addition to his throat cancer, Genet was suffering from a small hole in his foot. It was apparent in his walk. He limped. I had suggested he see an orthopaedic specialist. 'No,' he had replied, 'I can do what I like with this pain, I am holding on to it, it belongs to me'. He had spoken calmly, without aggression. It had made me remember his shock—his stupefaction mixed with constrained anger—when he had learnt he had cancer. In other words, it did not really matter to him that his heel bled and became infected, since the wound's existence was entirely within his control. Whereas with the cancer . . .

The cancer was part of his body that had escaped his control and—the pinnacle of humiliation and horror—inflicted an illness which he had believed reserved for the bourgeoisie.

Genet used to call me Dima. From his lips, my name, distorted but rapped out at top speed—Dima—sounded like a disorderly order, a joke. I liked that. I felt, in general, that with each thought, each stone, he killed two birds: iron discipline on the one hand and amusement and farce on the other. It would not have taken much for him to try and teach a bird to stand to attention. I also knew, I could feel, that the honeymoon period of that strange privilege—my tête-à-têtes with him—was under threat. I was an *impure* Arab in his eyes, I had the double 'handicap' of being born Christian, with a mother who was half-French to boot. The 'white' part of me bothered him. Worse—much worse—I claimed the right to criticize the political apparatus of the Palestinian Resistance, as much as anyone else. I was indeed up in arms against the Israeli government and against the militias of my community—the Maronites—but I also already had reasons to think that the PLO was replicating, in more than one respect, the failings and defects of many Arab regimes. Suffice to say that my crises of conscience— which were ultimately quite sterile—provided nothing of value for the love song of *Prisoner of Love*. Genet valued choosing the time and place of his mocking salvos and had good reason—and how—to protect their secret agenda. We probably owe his best pages on the Palestinians to this hijacking of reality, this theatrical heist of time and space. But in terms of the strictly political content of his writing, I tend to think that he only shone light—as Artaud said of life—'on his own suffering'. Let us just say that Genet's work is infinitely stronger when it takes a position of refusal and exile than one of common ground and unity. His *healthy* ideas are, for the most part, the escaped prey of his genius. A bit like childish tantrums which his humour, atrophied by sudden bursts of hate, seemed to have let by, or failed to notice. The Genet who is missed in these times of crippling sectarianism and moralizing is not, definitely not, the bitter author of 'The Criminal Child' or the indulgent witness of Stalin's regime and the Gulag. It is the thug, the poet, the gunslinger, the unswerving enemy of the 'strong'. He whose freedom was answerable only to itself and who, if he were alive today, would certainly have made use of that freedom to laugh in the face of those who have made it an excuse for war, a system of allegiance or a pitiful breath of air in a suffocating climate of surrender.

During the time I knew him, I wasn't quite sure what to do with the place he had provisionally granted me. It is even harder to deal, today, with an author whose territory is so locked down—closed, from one end to the other, behind the bars of a 'funereal' homosexuality. A universe which had no common cause with that of Gide, Proust, Jouhandeau, Wilde or countless others. Genet did not expand the field of writing to homosexuality. He turned his homosexuality and his fiction and plays into a single, unified creation: an erotic monument to death. He passed the handcuffs of his poetry around the wrists of his readers. So much so that on top of the enchantment—the poem—and the entrapment—the handcuffs—comes, for a woman, at least for me, the unnameable feeling of paying for access to that beauty by being served with an expulsion order. A feeling that degenerates into nausea, when, in *Funeral Rites*, for example, turning homosexuality against itself, he uses it as an instrument of torture against any symbol of love that is not connected with *droit de seigneur*, and with treason. And while Genet may lay this on out of sheer provocation and for aesthetic effect, this is the result: 'I am told that the German officer who was in charge of the Oradour butcher had a mild, rather likeable face. He did what he could—a great deal—for poetry. He deserved well of it. My deaths rarely express my cruelty. I love and respect that officer.'[14]

On more than one occasion, such words have made me feel like giving up on writing this book, running away from it.[15] If I keep going, it is because the self-portraits scattered throughout his work spare us from insult, pre-empting it brilliantly. As in *Funeral Rites*, again:

> I wanted to be a traitor, a thief, a robber, an informer, full of hate, a destroyer, full of scorn, a coward. With cries and axe blows, I cut the cords which attached me to the world of conventional morality, sometimes I carefully untied the knots. I made myself monstrous, separating myself from you, from your world and your institutions.[16]

No one could have said it better than he did: it makes no sense to claim to be on Genet's side. He certainly fought on the side of the oppressed, the weak and the dispossessed, but his struggle was not so much a struggle for

14 Jean Genet, *Funeral Rites* (Bernard Frechtman trans.) (New York: Grove Press, 1994), p. 215.

15 'Such words' does not imply that there are others of this nature on this topic. I mean rather to draw attention to Genet's sadistic exaggerations in general, whatever their object—himself included, of course.

16 Genet, *Funeral Rites*, p. 215.

justice as against injustice. A particular injustice. Justice in and of itself—he didn't care about solidarity. And, apart from some rare exceptions, he was more fervently attached to his enemies than to his friends. He said so himself. His writings on the Palestinians are in no way 'arguments' on one side or the other of the Palestinian question. Nonetheless, beyond their fundamentally subjective nature, his words represent an invaluable account of Palestinian and Arab society as witnessed in the 1970s and 80s. This is the unexpected paradox Genet presents. Who else—including among Arab authors—would have known how to flush out the corruption of those with power and wealth who were paving the way for Islamism, and the political chaos whose results we are now seeing, with such irony, precision and vision? Who else could have so accurately evoked the misery and the poetry that dwelt under the grim skies of the Palestinian camps, the terror inflicted on this people abruptly wrenched from their land, the unreal mixture of lightness and loneliness that hovered around the resistance fighters?

Let us say, to conclude—or, rather, before coming back to it—that being 'pro-Genet', thinking 'like Genet' is meaningless. What is exhilarating, however, is to begin one's thinking with him, because his position is exemplary. Exemplary 'in the special and paradoxical sense that it's unique, and will not serve as an example'.[17]

17 Jean Genet, *Prisoner of Love* (Barbara Bray trans.) (New York: New York Review of Books Classics, 2003), p. 301.

In a long, undated letter to Sartre, which was probably written in 1952, Genet wrote:

> From childhood on a trauma throws the soul into confusion. I think it happens like this: after a certain shock, I refuse to live. But, incapable of thinking about my death in clear, rational terms, I look at it symbolically by refusing to continue the world. Instinct then leads me toward my own sex. My pleasure will be *endless*. I will not embody the principle of continuity. It is a sulky attitude. . . . Slowly my psyche will propose to me funereal themes . . . These funereal themes, they too demand to be active, accomplished, if not there will be an explosion of madness! The proposed themes symbolic of death will thus be very narrow (the extraordinary limitation of the pederastic universe) (suicide, murder, theft, all anti-social acts, capable of giving me a death that if it isn't real is at least symbolic or social—prison). If one of these themes is *active*, in fact achieved, it will cause my death. Therefore it's necessary that I achieve it only in the imaginative realm . . . In any event the significance of homosexuality is this: a refusal to continue the world. Then, to alter sexuality. The child or adolescent who refuses the world and turns toward his own sex, knowing that he himself is a man, in struggling against this useless manliness is going to try to dissolve it, alter it;

there's only one way, which is to pervert it through pseudo-feminine behaviour. It's not, as people think, nostalgia about the idea of the woman one might have been which feminizes, rather it's the bitter need to mock virility.

. . . Significance of pederastic love: it's the possession of an object (the beloved) who will have no other fate than the fate of the lover. The beloved becomes the object ordained to 'represent' *death* (the lover) in life. That's why I want him to be handsome. He has the *visible* attributes when I will be dead. I commission him to live in my stead, my heir apparent. The beloved doesn't love me, he 'reproduces' me. But in this way I sterilize him, I cut him off from his own destiny.[18]

Genet does not cite Freud in his letter—citations are rare in his texts—but the choice of words, as elsewhere, leaves little doubt as to his importance.[19] An archive document

18 Jean Genet, Letter to Jean-Paul Sartre. Cited in Edmund White, *Genet: A Biography* (London: Vintage, 2004), pp. 440–2.

19 This is confirmed by the analysis he made, half a century later, of a line of Rimbaud's: his focus on the Freudian unconscious was neither superficial nor temporary. The line: 'O let my keel burst! Let me go to the sea!' Genet's analysis: 'What's surprising is that "O let my keel burst!"—the boat itself says that, the Drunken Boat, and in slang "keel" (*la quille*) means "leg." When he was seventeen, Rimbaud said: "O let my keel burst!" That is, "O let my leg . . . " And at thirty-seven he had his leg cut off, by the sea, at Marseille. That's all I wanted to say' (*The Declared Enemy*, pp. 188–9).

offers definitive proof. There is a handwritten response from Genet to a literary survey asking 'What place, what role in life, do you attribute to literature and the arts in 1935?' One passage by the twenty-four-year-old future author of *Our Lady of the Flowers* is of particular interest:

> Poe, Baudelaire, Novalis, followed by Rimbaud and Stephen George in literature, a Cubist/Dada movement and Freud above all, Freud the genius—without forgetting Bergson and his phi-losophy of intuition—seem to commit culture to the research of the unconscious. The truth, they tell us, is that our Self is not only the Self we know consciously. There is also a shadowy (it remains shadowy) sub-conscious. A morality—or rather, an amorality—will be born, have no doubt, from this new way of inquiring. The future is Freud's.[20]

Not only does Genet show a passion for the discovery of the unconscious, he is also already negotiating how he will appropriate and twist it. The amoral morality he tri-umphantly proclaims is clearly his own, and in no way that of Freud.

---

20 From the 1935 manuscript from the Fonds Genet de l'IMEC, pub-lished in the edition of *Europe* dedicated to Genet (August–September 1996). The origin and context of the three-part questionnaire, which called, at the bottom of the page, for 'human expression, not a scholarly text', are unknown [our translation].

Fifty years after his letter to Sartre, Genet evoked the 'gift of prophecy about oneself' which led Rimbaud to predict the amputation of his leg twenty years before the event.[21] I now find myself wondering about a similar point in regard to Genet. The heavy smoker who had cancer of the throat, rather than the lung. Avoid 'madness and choking', he wrote to Sartre. Madness, yes—Genet did not stop at avoiding it, he drove it away, banned it, made no concessions to it. Not even in his theatrical works, where no fool or madman is to be found. Mastery and control were, from beginning to end, the pillars of his thought, and even of his lyricism. 'Poetry is wilful,' he wrote in *Our Lady of the Flowers*.

The effect of swelling and obstruction in the throat—I wonder if he was not its prey and victim, at the end of his life, if this was not the price of his choice: such a great will to power in such a great absence of madness. In this respect, he was the opposite of his poetic counterparts, Artaud and Nietzsche.

The throat. Few poets have given as much life to the verb 'to sing' as Genet. 'I want to sing the murderer, since I like murderers. Sing them without softening the edges,' he wrote in prison. 'I know of no criteria for the beauty of an act, an object or a being other than the song it kindles within me.'

21 See note 15.

Will it be said that I'm singing? I am. I sing Mettray, our prisons and my hoodlums, to whom I secretly give the pretty name 'petty tyrants.' Your song has no object. You sing the void. Words may conjure up for you the pirate I want to speak of. To me he remains invisible. The face of him who commanded the ship of troubles my childhood is forever lost to me, and in order to speak accurately to you about him I have a right to use as a model a handsome German soldier—I even desire him—who shot a bullet into the charming neck of a fifteen-year-old kid and who returned to his barracks no less clean, no less pure, heroized even more by that useless murder.[22]

This extract from *Miracle of the Rose* can be read as one likes: as a poem, as an affront, as a joke, or as all three at once. In my case, I see it, in addition and most importantly, as the most intimate of confessions coupled with a strong dose of deceit. The kind of swindle no one did better than Genet and which included, to give one example, passing off the pervert he was for a monster he wasn't. Besides, throughout his work it is the 'feints' of the conman and the snippets of information he gives about himself directly which tell us most about the motivations behind his provocations and his acts of bravado, how much truth there was

---

22 Genet, *Miracle of the Rose*, p. 79 [translation modified]. The following quotes are from the same source.

in them and what was really going on behind the scenes. This little phrase is a specific example: 'The face of him who commanded the ship of troubles my childhood is forever lost to me'. Without these silencing words, which leave an 'empty space [*un blanc*]' in the middle of the tirade and at the same time displace the words that follow into the realm of pure fantasy, the whole would make no sense. Yet for Genet, this metaphor which evokes the invisible pirate, the forever unnameable father, is once again central: it is a reverse image of the world, the place where death gives birth to life. From which comes desire's blind riposte to absence, a crime made into a poem, the choice of the handsome German soldier, the pointless murder of a fifteen-year-old kid or the simultaneous sabotage of self by father and father by self. Or, further, the out-and-out war waged by one man against the world. The boy and the soldier work together to close off escape routes and to recommence playing out a scenario in which they are frenzied images, without reflections. We will never know how much violence Genet did himself in order to inflict it upon others. However, I am almost certain that his address to the tightrope-walker was the most accurate of his self-portraits:

> Artificially, by an act of willpower, you will have to allow that lack of feeling towards the world enter into you. As its waves rise in you—like the cold, starting at the feet, climbed up the legs, the thighs and the stomach of Socrates—their

coldness grips your heart and freezes it . . . At the same time a sort of vapour must escape from you, a light vapour which does not blur your edges, showing us that at your centre a fire never stops feeding that icy death which entered into you through your feet.

A little further on:

We didn't come to the circus to see a whore, but a solitary lover pursuing his own image, which flees out of reach and vanishes on a metal wire.

'It is an awful torment that makes you dance,' he wrote. 'The audience sees only fire and, believing you are simply playing, not knowing that you are the fire-raiser, they applaud the fire.'[23] Like the dancer in whom he saw his own image, or, rather, who fatally corresponded to his dreams, Genet came onstage 'with such sumptuous make-up that his entrance immediately provoked nausea', knowing that he could only depend on the beauty of his voice for his salvation, the empty air screwed by words.[24] His voice must have been to his song what the wire is to the dance of the tightrope-walker. The tomb of an angel turned into the throat of the devil, spitting its mesmerizing barrage in the invented face of a faceless audience. Coincidence or fate?

23 Jean Genet, *Oeuvres complètes*, VOL. 5, *Le funambule*; *Le secret de Rembrandt* (Paris : Gallimard, 1979), p. 21 [our translation].
24 Ibid.

It happened that it was exactly there, at the scene of the crime, in his throat, in the place where death, freshly warmed, would evaporate, giving birth to his song, that a cancerous tumour lodged, a few years before his death.

Parricide. If the work of any other author shines light on Genet's, it is that of Dostoevsky, though in some ways it is the polar opposite of his own. Especially *The Brothers Karamazov*. While the author of *Funeral Rites* granted it the status of 'masterpiece of the novel, a great book, a bold instigation of souls', he immediately sought to twist its meaning and make us share his 'wish to laugh in the face of the false and very real imposture that is its destiny'. 'Dostoyevsky,' he continues, 'at last completes something that would make him supreme: a farce, a piece of buffoonery at once enormous and petty, and since it is exercised over everything that made him such a possessed novelist, it is exercised against himself, and with shrewd and childlike methods, which he uses with the stubborn bad faith of Saint Paul.'[25] What kind of conflict provoked such a *brief* diagnosis from Genet, such blatant evasiveness? Here, every action 'has a meaning and an opposite meaning,' he writes: 'For the first time, it seems to me, the psychological explanation is destroyed by another (opposite) psychological explanation. The actions or intentions that we have a habit—in books and even in daily life—of considering as

25 Genet, *The Declared Enemy*, p. 182.

wicked lead to salvation, and kindly acts and intentions provoke catastrophe.'[26] It is difficult to believe that these are Genet's words. Genet, the master of ambivalence, thinking that 'two opposing explanations' results in a draw, a 'good joke'? The genius and vision of the Russian— which consisted of making right and wrong, good and evil, faith and unbelief coexist, as in life, at the heart of a single individual, a single thought, a single action—must have rattled the untouchable and unyielding Genet, shaking him and making him lose his footing. And in his own literary domain to boot: in the writing of evil.

But—dramatically—in the last lines of these few pages concerning the Karamazovs, Genet strikes back with a question that clouds everything he has just said. Suddenly, from underneath the arrogance and disrespect, the voice of a wounded child pierces through. The question, which is yet to be answered, is as follows:

And Smerdyakov?

Because there are four of them, the three brothers Karamazov. The gentle Christian Alyosha doesn't say a single word, doesn't make one gesture, to show that this worm is his brother.

I'd like to talk about Smerdyakov.[27]

---

26 Ibid., p. 183.
27 Ibid., p. 185.

This is how the text ends. Why Smerdyakov? Why the special attention towards the 'worm'? And above all, why did Genet, having started down that path, abruptly stop? The fact that Smerdyakov is a murderer and a bastard—and, moreover, the son of a maid—is certainly important, but it is not enough of an explanation. Genet would not have bothered himself over so little. The answer lies, I feel, in Smerdyakov's actual character, in the strange combination of the inferiority of his existence and the superiority of his cunning. The rotten fruit of a rotten life, he kills another and kills himself, but falsehood and truth, tried one after the other, serve him no purpose. His vengeance brings him only a few wretched moments of pleasure, lived between two hells, between slow death and suicide. Smerdyakov's crime is, to put it mildly, without genius, without reward, 'lost' to poetry, so to speak. In a sense this man is the anti-Genet. He is the alternative image Genet could have been expected to become, whose fate he brilliantly escaped. Nonetheless, confronted with the other three—the 'legitimate' brothers—Genet looks out for the brat, he is on his side. He would never stray from this loyalty. It served, across his entire life, as a counterweight to his betrayals. And his reasoning, when referring specifically to Smerdyakov, is unanswerable: Alyosha, the good, the pure Alyosha who devotes himself to others without thinking, who flies to the rescue of sinners and the dying, who transforms evil into good, sin into forgiveness, the devil into God, how can it be that he does not lift a finger for Smerdyakov? Dostoevsky said everything there was to be said in that sublime and terrible novel—almost everything, everything except that. It is not surprising that this hole in the canvas should have been noticed by one who did not so much spend his time penetrating people's souls as seeking out the lie skulking under goodness and extolling the beauty that comes out of evil.

To Marya Kondratyevna, who has just flattered him with the words 'How clever you are! How is it you've gone so deep into everything?', how does Smerdyakov reply?

> I could have done better than that. I could have known more than that, if it had not been for my destiny from my childhood up. I would have shot a man in a duel if he called me names because I am descended from a filthy beggar and have no father . . . I would have sanctioned their killing me before I was born that I might not have come into the world at all. They used to say in the market, and your mamma too, with great lack of delicacy, set off telling me that her hair was like a mat on her head, and that she was short of five foot by a wee bit . . . I hate all Russia, Marya Kondratyevna.[28]

And what did Genet reply to the German writer, Hubert Fichte, when the latter asked him, 'And this fascination,

---

28 Fyodor Dostoevsky, *The Brothers Karamazov* (Constance Garnett trans.) (Calgary: Theophania, 2005), p. 187.

which was so bewildering to me, this admiration for assas-
sins, for Hitler, for the concentration camps—all this has
drained away?'

> What did it mean, this fascination for brutes or
> assassins or Hitler? In more direct and perhaps
> also simpler terms, I remind you that I was an
> orphan, I was raised by Public Welfare, I found
> out very early on that I wasn't French and that I
> didn't belong to the village . . . oh! the word isn't
> too strong, to hate France is nothing, you have to
> do more than hate, more than loathe France,
> finally I . . . and . . . the fact that the French army,
> the most prestigious thing in the world thirty
> years ago, that they surrendered to the troops of
> an Austrian corporal, well, to me that was
> absolutely thrilling.[29]

One hated Russia, the other hated France. One, who
stuck to the story of his filiation on his mother's side
(Smerdyastchaya means 'stinking' in Russian) persisted in
being 'ignorant' that he was the son of Karamazov, the
other, who left behind the French identity of his mother,
Camille Genet, stubbornly believed, without any proof,
that his father was not French. Both dreamt of seeing their
country on its knees. Smerdyakov says so, as does Genet:

> 'I don't want to be a hussar, Marya Kondratyevna,
> and, what's more, I should like to abolish all
> soldiers.'

29 Genet, *The Declared Enemy*, pp. 125–6.

'And when an enemy comes, who is going to defend us?'

'There's no need of defence. In 1812 there was a great invasion of Russia by Napoleon, first Emperor of the French, father of the present one, and it would have been a good thing if they had conquered us. A clever nation would have conquered a very stupid one and annexed it. We should have had quite different institutions.'[30]

However unorthodox it may be to establish a connection between an author and a character from the novel of a different author, it has turned out to be at once a more enlightening and more troubling technique than I had expected. For the kinship between Genet and Smerdyakov does not end there. In the same interview—many years before Genet wrote his text on *The Brothers Karamazov*—Frichte asked him, 'Are there other literary works that impressed you as much as Proust's did?' And Genet replied:

Oh, of course! Some even more than that. There's *The Brothers Karamazov* . . . for me, nothing equals *The Brothers Karamazov*. There are so many different times involved. There was the time of Sonia and the time of Ilyusha, there was the time of Smerdyakov, and then there was my own time of reading. There was the time of deciphering, and

---

30 Dostoevsky, *The Brothers Karamazov*, p. 187.

then there was the time that came before their appearance in the book. What was Smerdyakov doing before being spoken of?[31]

Sonia, Ilyusha and . . . Smerdyakov. Smerdyakov again, and again a question without an answer. Not only does Genet resolutely refrain from citing the names of the three brothers (Ivan, Dimitri and Alyosha), not that that should come as a surprise—but he confuses the woman's name (no surprise there either): there is no Sonia in the novel.[32] His connection with the Karamazovs is more than subjective, it is truly passionate. It doesn't take much imagination to see him prowling through stubbornly debating with Ivan, provoking Mitya's enmity, ridiculing Alyosha, and, while we're on the subject, testifying against the three of them, that is to say, sharing in the crime and standing by Smerdyakov. And the latter, indeed, 'What was he doing before being spoken of?' He appears at the start of Chapter Two, which is devoted to his mother, Elisabeth Smerdyastchaya, a wretched orphan who inspires a well-to-do young man with this question, tossed out to his companions like a challenge: Could anyone 'possibly look upon such an animal as a woman'? Fyodor Pavlovitch, the father of the Karamazovs, who is with the group, 'declared that it was by

31 Genet, The Declared Enemy, pp. 141–2 [translation modified].

32 Genet is doubtlessly thinking of young Sonia from Crime and Punishment (1866), Raskolnikov's loving and humble saviour.

no means impossible'. 'Five or six months later, all the town was talking, with intense and sincere indignation, of Lizaveta's condition.' The young woman gives birth to Smerdyakov and dies at dawn, near the Karamazov house. He is taken in by the servant couple, who lost their own malformed baby at birth.

Grigory took the baby, brought it home and, making his wife sit down, put it on her lap. 'A child of God—an orphan is akin to all,' he said, 'and to us above others. Our little lost one has sent us this, who has come from the devil's son and a holy innocent. Nurse him and weep no more.'[33]

As he pored over the book, Genet too bound himself to the son of the 'devil and a holy innocent', creating a connection that defies commentary. Dostoevsky dealt with the fate of the child without further ado, simply letting us know, without filling in the intervening details, that he became Fyodor Pavlovitch Karamazov's cook. 'I ought to say something of this Smerdyakov,' he ends the page, 'but I am ashamed of keeping my readers' attention so long occupied with these common menials, and I will go back to my story, hoping to say more of Smerdyakov in the course of it.' And so he passes over the bastard's first twenty-four years in silence. A fact of utmost importance to Genet, who, having chosen his man and his side, finds himself, in the novel as in his life, cut off from his origins.

---

33 Dostoevsky, *The Brothers Karamazov*, p. 81.

At what point and in what way does Smerdyakov return in the narrative? With an order from the head of the Karamazov household, who, after having offered his son Alyosha a liqueur, says 'Smerdyakov, go to the cupboard, the second shelf on the right. Here are the keys. Look sharp!'

And what happens a moment later? In the grip of one of his excitable, unbalanced, aggravated moods, the father says to the son 'Now we've a treat for you, in your own line, too. It'll make you laugh. Balaam's ass has begun talking to us here—and how he talks! How he talks!' And Dostoevsky continues: 'Balaam's ass, it appeared, was the valet, Smerdyakov. He was a young man of about four and twenty, remarkably unsociable and taciturn. Not that he was shy or bashful. On the contrary, he was conceited and seemed to despise everybody.'[34]

'Are you a human being? . . . You're not a human being. You grew from the mildew in the bath-house . . . ,' Grigory had said to Smerdyakov as a child. He used to be 'very fond of hanging cats, and burying them with great ceremony'. Not words to forget. One day when Grigory is teaching the boy the Scriptures, the latter begins to laugh. 'What's that for?' asks Grigory, looking at him threateningly from under his spectacles. 'Oh, nothing. God created light on the first day, and the sun, moon, and stars on the fourth day. Where did the light come from on the first day?'[35]

34 Ibid., p. 101.
35 Ibid., p. 102.

The wording of the reply, the ironic and *detached* tone, fiercely logical and faux-inquisitive, the icy mixture of feigned naivety and precision, is a perfect likeness—this is pure Genet! Smerdyakov addresses the others present, the elder Karamazov, Alyosha, Grigory and Ivan, who has arrived in the meantime. Like a good casuist, he makes use of every possible argument to defend his contention that it is better to deny one's faith and save one's skin than to die under the torture of those who demand you renounce it. Here I cannot help but think of a phrase of Genet's. It is to Smerdyakov's words what a masterfully painted portrait is to its subject:

> If I were told that I was risking death in refusing to cry '*Vive la France*', I would cry it in order to save my hide, but I would cry softly. If I had to cry it very loudly, I would do so, but laughingly, without believing in it. And if I had to believe in it, I would; then I would immediately die of shame.[36]

Yet I have probably been too quick, much too quick, to think that in Genet's view Smerdyakov's suicidal vengeance can be reduced to an act 'without reward'. In the end, it is he, the 'worm' who derails everything. It is he who succeeds, with a single stroke, in precipitating the slaughter of the Karamazov family. Not only the death of the father and the unjust conviction of Mitya, the eldest son, but also

36 Genet, *Funeral Rites*, p. 32.

the damnation of the intellectual hero, the moralist: Ivan Karamazov. Ivan's ramblings in the final pages of the novel, when he is bedridden at Smerdyakov's—who, in each of their conversations, leads him astray, strings him along, tortures him and only eventually decides to spit the truth at him in order to further confuse him—must have made Genet laugh as he read them. Even as at the thought of Ivan Fyodorovitch's face when the servant shows his cards: 'And so I want to prove to your face this evening that you are the only real murderer in the whole affair, and I am not the real murderer, though I did kill him. You are the rightful murderer.'[37] One could easily picture this truth-seeker, spared any dishonour, who suddenly finds himself caught in the web of his lies, unmasked by a worm, whose intelligence he is forced to recognize, within Genet's plays. 'No, you are not a fool,' Ivan tells him, terrified, during their third conversation, 'you are far cleverer than I thought . . .' Of course, Smerdyakov is driven to suicide, but Ivan's fate is worse. Condemned by his brother's servant to recognize his own cowardice and venality—his share in the crime— he loses more than his life, he loses his reason. This posthumous revenge taken by cunning and suffering on the powers of justice and logic is a victory for the author of *The Screens* and *Our Lady of the Flowers*. There remains only one question to be answered. Why was his text on the Karamazovs left 'incomplete', unfinished? Why did he

37 Dostoevsky, *The Brothers Karamazov*, p. 583.

mention Smerdyakov so often without telling us what he truly thought? 'I would read one page, and then . . . I'd have to think for two hours, then start again, it's enormous, and it's exhausting,' he told Fichte.[38] He ultimately resolved this exhausting reflection, which left no possibility of separating good and evil, by returning it, like a letter, to its sender: 'Did I read *The Brothers Karamazov* badly? I read it as a joke.'[39] It is not difficult to imagine that Genet only partially relished Ivan's fall. After all, the author of the *Grand Inquisitor* dream also pleased him in some ways. This left him with a conundrum, an impossible question, which in the end he neatly sidestepped: 'I read it as a joke.' After all, was not the only real victory, in Genet's eyes, the defeat of 'good' Alyosha? The character whom Dostoevsky had originally wanted to make the central hero of the novel, as a martyr. Luckily for us, he too is 'overcome' by the powerful pull of evil. Even he is not allowed, in his inner life, to let 'goodness' occupy centrestage so easily.

Let us imagine, to conclude, that this work—*The Brothers Karamazov*—was only a 'farce' in Genet's eyes, that he was convinced he could reduce it to this simple fact: 'everything—characters, events, everything—means one thing *and* also its opposite, nothing is left but tatters.'[40] If this is the case,

38 Genet, *The Declared Enemy*, p. 123.

39 Ibid., p. 184.

40 Ibid. [translation modified].

why does he consider certain characters more important, Smerdyakov and Alyosha in particular?

If there was an author capable of putting Genet on the spot, of checking his omnipotence, of breaking through his defences, even if only for the duration of his reading (two months for *The Brothers Karamazov*), it was without doubt the author of *The House of the Dead* (1862), the former convict who was well acquainted with madness, imprisonment and brutality and who, without the least interest in any aesthetics of evil, took the novel to the greatest heights without worrying about 'style' in the sense that Genet used it. And, on this subject, is it a coincidence that the latter abandoned style when he came to write about the Karamazovs? Composed in crude, staccato language, these few pages have no precedent in his writing. 'Form is the essence brought to the surface,' said Victor Hugo. Yes, but in Dostoevsky's novels, the essence is everywhere, the surface nowhere. This could not have failed to touch Genet. He had built his written work—his general relationship with words—on music and on the infallible grasp of the depths through form; here he shows signs of willingly letting go. Or at least trying to. The introduction of his text on *The Brothers Karamazov* is something of a direct admission. He writes:

> Artistic or poetic works of art are the highest form of the human spirit, its most convincing expression: that is a commonplace that should be filed

under the rubric 'eternal truth'. Whether they are the highest form of the human spirit, or the highest form given to the human spirit, or the highest form taken, patiently or quickly, by a lucky chance, but always boldly, it is a question of a form, and this form is far from being the limit to which a human can venture.[41]

This question of form—of its at once decisive and arbitrary character—can be read, between the lines, as a private conversation between Genet and Genet. 'Far from being the limit to which a human can venture': a strange phrase which, read literally, implies madness or crime. However, in this context it signifies that with his final novel Dostoevsky seemingly pushed the boundaries beyond what is conventionally known as 'form', and signals that Genet too is preparing himself, at death's door, for a new understanding of writing. Which would, in fact, be the case with *Prisoner of Love*, the most polymorphous of his works, teeming with every kind of metamorphosis, where humour, ostentation and splendour, jewels and dross, transparency and pomposity coexist, in their utmost extremes. The best and the worst of Jean Genet. The best, when his intelligence serves as a compass for his creative genius; the worst when, becoming an end in itself, his intelligence overdoes the artifice and adds one mask too many. So much so that the description Genet gives of

41 Ibid., p. 182.

Dostoevsky's 'late style' seems to me, all things considered, to apply more to his own than to the Russian's: 'After each chapter, we're sure: there's no truth left . . . Masterly humour. Game. But risky, because it destroys the *dignity* of the narrative.'[42]

Sartre said as much in relation to *Funeral Rites*: 'Jean and Genet vanish together on the last page of the book, along with Erik and Riton, who embody them. The result is zero. The work cancels out: there were only dead leaves.'[43]

As with exaggeration in a Fellini film or a Kafka novel, a pattern of oppositions is sometimes the easiest way to grasp nuance. I feel this is the case with Dostoevsky and Genet. The firmly contradictory responses which these two writers, obsessed with crime, give to the question of evil allow us to examine—from every side—the repercussions of guilt or lack of guilt for the fate of thought. In other words, the autobiographical roots of all moral convictions. And since we are concerned here with Genet's in particular, the autobiographical roots of his *immoral* moralism.

One of them, Dostoevsky, coming from a family of eight children, had a cruel, brutal, bad-tempered, arrogant and

42 Ibid., p. 184.

43 Jean-Paul Sartre, *Saint Genet* (Bernard Frechtman trans.) (Minneapolis: University of Minnesota Press, 2012), p. 540.

miserly man for a father, who would, as we know, be murdered by his muzhiks. The other, an only child, had no
father, nor the slightest idea what his father had been like.
The first had a sweet, affectionate woman for a mother, a
lover of poetry, who was also probably depressed and certainly unhappy and who, tormented by her husband's jealous fits, would die of consumption two years before him.
The second had a young, unmarried mother, who as far as
we can tell was defenceless and poor, destitute in every
respect. She abandoned him after seven months, with the
name of a flower: Genet.[44] The Russian, who belonged to
an old noble family on his father's side, spent his childhood
in Moscow in a house attached to the hospital where his
father worked as a doctor. The Frenchman was entrusted
by the Assistance publique to foster parents—a peasant
family in the Morvan region. He lost his adoptive mother,
Eugénie, at the age of eleven. This death, which he passed
over in silence in his writing, definitely helped push him
towards exile from the world and its laws. At the age of
eighteen, Dostoevsky learnt of his father's murder and
soon after had his first attack of epilepsy. He told his friends
that for his entire life the moment preceding an attack was
one of heavenly exaltation. Freud interpreted the situation
in these terms: 'In the aura of the epileptic attack, one
moment of supreme bliss is experienced. This may very
well be a record of the triumph and sense of liberation felt

44 French for 'broom'. [Trans]

on hearing the news of the death, to be followed immediately by an all the more cruel punishment.'[45]

Around the same age, having been in prison in Meaux as well as a stint in Mettray penal colony, Genet enlisted, committing himself to two years in the army without waiting for the call-up. 'Creating always means talking about childhood,' he would say forty years later. The author of *The Brothers Karamazov*, who would probably not have rejected such a statement, fulfilled his father's wishes at the age of twenty-two by graduating as an engineer, and started to write. One thing is certain: as he left adolescence, Genet declared war on the world and loudly declared himself free of any form of guilt. Dostoevsky, on the contrary, was racked by blame, remorse and punishment. Both were obsessed with the father. Both were obsessed by crime and the desire to kill. Genet, whose father was invisible, impossible to kill in person, delegated his crime to his lovers, his future heroes, who were, and will remain, characters of Genet himself rather than simply belonging in his novels. And to the extent that parricide—the murder of the father, as embodied by the world—was for him only ever a beginning, inevitably an impossible goal, any inhibition or regret was nullified in advance. All that mattered was the beauty

45 Sigmund Freud, 'Dostoevsky and Parricide' (1928) in *The Standard Edition of the Complete Psychological Works of Sigmund Freud* (James Strachey trans., in collaboration with Anna Freud), VOL. 21 (London: Hogarth Press / The Institute of Psycho-analysis, 1961), pp. 177–94; here, p. 186.

of the act. Dostoevsky, who on the contrary felt his father's presence only too keenly, sowed his evil all around, and his efforts brought forth a forest of monsters haunted by angels. Of all their differences, the greatest is the way they relate to the murdered: for Genet, the celebration is caused, rather than interrupted, by the bereavement. For him, death is a condition of life, its proof. For Dostoevsky, it is the opposite: death punishes life for having rejoiced in it, it castrates life. From there—through them, through their meeting—the question that every human being must ask emerges: that of the continuation of life in death. Not the death of a person's loved one or the mourning of the other, but the death of the self which is specifically produced by the Oedipal desire for the death of the father. 'One has wished another person dead, and now one is this other person and is dead oneself,' stated Freud in his introduction to *The Brothers Karamazov*.

This death of the self, as we have seen, was given to Genet— he gave it to himself—at birth. For him, life and survival, killer and victim, father and son absorb each other from the beginning. And this fusion / destruction is the spark for his genius: death, animated, eroticized, transformed into life. 'The author of a beautiful poem is always dead,' he wrote, aged thirty, in *Miracle of the Rose*. 'Inside me lay the corpse I'd been for a long while,' he would write again, forty-five years later, in *Prisoner of Love*. 'What surprises me,' he continues, 'is how still it lay, despite air pockets, sudden starts, high seas, bumps and broken propellers. Everything jolted along, and me with it, a parcel and at the same time a human being, a name and a tomb, a parcel and a corpse, eating, looking, laughing, whistling and loving left, right and centre.'[46]

From the beginning of his destiny to the end, dead-Genet played living-Genet. This reversal—a corpse giving birth to his existence—is the basis for his tremendous capacity for inverting all values and calmly plundering all the assets of existence and thought. He projects the same solitude—his own—onto both the author of death *and* the one who receives it. This projection gives him not only the 'innate' right to lovingly celebrate the murderer but also to bring together, even to merge, his fate with that of his victim. If life produces a corpse, death, lending its breath, gives it a meaning, warms it up, turns it on. One is nothing without the other. Which, for him, is where the sexual fantasy's absolute power comes from: in Genet's homosexuality, life does not fuck death; the sensation of death arouses life, penetrates it, brings it to orgasm. This is also at the root of his work's lack of metaphysical angst. His heaven was more of a pagan theatre of earthly games of life and death than a separate, bodiless world. Any 'realist' reading of his veneration of crime inevitably comes up against a gaping 'absence of reality': the same absence that grounds Genet's birth and motivates his retaliation.

46 Genet, *Prisoner of Love*, p. 219.

However monstrous they may be, his murderers are only ever partially so: their crimes form an aura around them rather than possessing them. This is clear from the difference, the disparity, between criminals and crimes in his work. Criminals abound, they are everywhere. Crimes, on the other hand, are very rare.[47] Barely mentioned, barely described, conjured away like a magician's handkerchief. Time after time Genet gives his characters an order to kill, and time after time the victim disappears in a puff of smoke before they have the chance to stir our emotions. The victim is nobody, is absent. Their dying moments? Almost nothing. A hand letting go of a puppet. A circus gesture. Neither guilty of the crime nor sensitized to the victim's misfortune, the reader does not so much owe their discomfort to the killer's cruelty as to Genet's: his relentless absence of pity, his unbending and icy humour. As he writes, he marries together the most improbable couple—obscenity and grace. Genet once said to me, 'When Abdallah died, I suffered from my lack of pain.'[48] Perhaps also he had suffered too much to be able to bear that it had not killed him. At any rate, dead-Genet never stopped taking

---

47 *Querelle of Brest* (1947), the most dramatic of his novels, is an exception to the rule. And even then . . . only up to a point. I will deal with this further on.

48 Abdallah Bentaga, a circus tightrope-walker, was Genet's lover at the end of the 1950s. He twice fell from the wire, in 1959 and 1961, before giving up the act for good. Abandoned by Genet, he committed suicide in February 1964. See White, *Genet*.

possession of living-Genet's suffering (an idea that comes not from him or from me but from his work). It occurs to me to wonder if this 'suffering born of not suffering' is also a suffering he wanted to pass on to us—his readers—except that, as an additional torment, he also inflicted upon us the final *délicatesse* (his favourite word) of the terrible harmony he created between horror and poetry. If I had to sum up the most troubling aspect of Genet's work in one sentence, I would say that I feel it lies in the creation of that 'harmony': in that 'enclosed' moment during which—the music permitting the perversion to take place—hell and beauty reside in exactly the same place.

Not only did Dostoevsky want nothing to do with such a coexistence, his novels are entirely dedicated to combating it. For the author of *The Brothers Karamazov* and *Demons* (1872), beauty could never be a way out. In fact, the opposite was more likely: it was the enemy, the danger. 'Beauty is a terrible and awful thing,' says Mitya, torn between love and dissoluteness, to his younger brother, Alyosha.

> It is terrible because it has not been fathomed and never can be fathomed, for God sets us nothing but riddles . . . Too many riddles weigh men down on earth. We must solve them as we can, and try to keep a dry skin in the water. Beauty! I can't endure the thought that a man of lofty mind and heart begins with the ideal of the Madonna and ends with the ideal of Sodom. What's still more

awful is that a man with the ideal of Sodom in his soul does not renounce the ideal of the Madonna ... The devil only knows what to make of it! What to the mind is shameful is beauty and nothing else to the heart.[49]

Such beauty, as well as its torments—this advantage of the devil's in his duel with God—is fundamental for the author of *Our Lady of the Flowers*. Once more, the Russian's contagious 'terror'—his self torn between faith and disbelief, elevation and degradation, the heavens and the abyss—is at the opposite extreme to Genet's solitary 'terrorism'. The criminal lauded by the latter is 'the conscious, even cynical murderer, who dares take it upon himself to deal death without trying to refer his acts to some power of a given order, for the soldier who kills does not assume responsibility, nor does the lunatic, nor the jealous man, nor the one who knows he will be forgiven.'[50]

His 'lost man' is a 'creator' who takes life away just as God grants it, without precedent and without support. 'The murderer compels my respect,' he writes, 'not only because he has known a rare experience, but because he has set himself up as a god, on an altar, whether of shaky boards or azure air.'[51]

49 Dostoevsky, *The Brothers Karamazov*, p. 88.
50 Genet, *Our Lady of the Flowers*, p. 121.
51 Ibid.

This is the very opposite of Raskolnikov, the criminal of *Crime and Punishment*, who unquestionably falls prey to madness and jealousy. He does, certainly, have bouts of cynicism and disdain for the morality of 'halfpenny philosophers', right up until almost the end, that is, up until he starts his life in the penal colony.

> He was ashamed just because he, Raskolnikov, had so hopelessly, stupidly come to grief through some decree of blind fate, and must humble himself and submit to 'the idiocy' of a sentence, if he were anyhow to be at peace.

Or:

> 'Why does my action strike them as so horrible?' he said to himself. 'Is it because it was a crime? What is meant by crime? My conscience is at rest. Of course, it was a legal crime, of course, the letter of the law was broken and blood was shed. Well, punish me for the letter of the law . . . and that's enough.'[52]

But his torment and his febrility inevitably destroy all the cold constructs of his reason, leaving him, despite his efforts, filled with a crazed impulse, a wild will to live. His 'resistance', his rational justifications for his crime, are defeated in the end, crushed by what Genet held in horror: expiation, the search for forgiveness. 'Life had stepped into

---

52 Fyodor Dostoevsky, *Crime and Punishment* (Constance Garnett trans.); available at: http://goo.gl/WEGLF6 (last accessed on 29 October 2015).

the place of theory,' Dostoevsky concludes on the very last page of the novel. Of course, his criminal still has seven years in Siberia to serve, but he is rehabilitated, saved *in extremis*. He is 'renewed by love'. The Christian love of Sonia.

Indeed, but despite the book's happy ending, the 'arguments' Raskolnikov puts to himself, the arguments which, in a sense, lead to his downfall, are neither countered nor overcome. They conserve a timeless force which tampers with the improvised 'miracle' of the ending's intentions, a force which sounds the death knell of 'morality's' conventions and, in common with Nietzsche, eradicates the boundaries between good and evil. His reasoning? He divided people into two categories, '[one] inferior (ordinary), that is, so to say, material that serves only to reproduce its kind, and men who have the gift or the talent to utter *a new word*'.[53] An individual of the latter kind 'can, I maintain, find within himself, in his conscience, a sanction for wading through blood,' he clarifies. 'All . . . well, legislators and leaders of men, such as Lycurgus, Solon, Mahomet, Napoleon, and so on, were all without exception

53 He continues: 'The first category, generally speaking, are men conservative in temperament and law-abiding; they live under control and love to be controlled. To my thinking it is their duty to be controlled, because that's their vocation, and there is nothing humiliating in it for them. The second category all transgress the law; they are destroyers or disposed to destruction according to their capacities' (ibid.).

criminals, from the very fact that, making a new law, they transgressed the ancient one.'

'I fail to understand,' he says to his sister Dounia, 'why bombarding people by regular siege is more honourable than killing someone with an axe.'[54] This question, which never ceased to obsess Dostoevsky, is dismissed without hesitation by Genet. Unlike Raskolnikov, his criminal does not seek to carve out a path for himself among men. He answers to himself and himself only. In this respect, 'he', the murderer, and he, Genet, converge in a single, identical will.

Not without reason does one, Dostoevsky, give the readers every tiny detail of Raskolnikov's double murder[55] while the other, Genet, half-executioner, half-conjurer, delivers Querelle's crimes with an irrefutable gesture, with just two words. For Raskolnikov—tormented, persecuted by his

---

54 Ibid. [translation modified].

55 'The old woman was as always bareheaded. Her thin, light hair, streaked with grey, thickly smeared with grease, was plaited in a rat's tail and fastened by a broken horn comb which stood out on the nape of her neck. As she was so short, the blow fell on the very top of her skull. She cried out, but very faintly, and suddenly sank all of a heap on the floor, raising her hands to her head . . . In the middle of the room stood Lizaveta with a big bundle in her arms. She was gazing in stupefaction at her murdered sister . . . And this hapless Lizaveta was so simple and had been so thoroughly crushed and scared that she did not even raise a hand to guard her face . . . The axe fell with the sharp edge just on the skull and split at one blow all the top of the head' (ibid.).

conscience—nothing is ever enough. No suffering, no proof can satisfy his thirst or exhaust his reserves of remorse and guilt. For Querelle, conscience and the unconscious are bound together. Together they control the ebb and flow of the soul, close off exits and force reality to march to their time. They do not deal with the world, but without it and against it. They require space and balance. For the song to flow forth, for the murderer to dance, the crime must be light, lively, *bright*. It must be clear and relentless, barely real. Musical. Sade celebrated by Mozart. A fantasy.

Far more than the French word *fantasme*, the English word fantasy best expresses the essence of writing and crime as Genet sees them: his way of negotiating the survival of the image after death. Such is the scene of the murder of the Armenian by Querelle, the sailor from Brest. 'The scene is Beirut', we learn, bluntly, at the beginning of a paragraph.[56] Querelle and Jonas, another sailor, meet a man walking past the brothel they are leaving. They don't have a cent between them. 'Him? He's a queer. There's no mistaking his sort,' says Jonas, 'They're usually rolling in it, a lot more than us, the pricks.'[57] Scene One: Querelle lets Jonas have the prey. The prey's name is Joachim, he's

---

56 Jean Genet, *Querelle of Brest* (Gregory Steatham trans.) (London: Faber & Faber, 2000), p. 208.

57 Ibid., p. 209 [translation modified].

already had his eyes on Querelle and he speaks French with words as colourful, as bedecked with flowers, ribbons, mother-of-pearl and mauve cushions as his bedroom will be, two pages later. 'I am Armenian. But I am so thoroughly French at heart. For me, France is Corneille and the divine Verlaine. I was educated at a Marist Mission School. Now I'm in business. I sell soft drinks . . . fizzy lemonade.'[58]

The meeting ends abruptly. Jonas demands they go to the seafront, the man wants them to go to his place. Their paths separate. The curtain falls. Ten minutes later, 'the Armenian . . . ran slap up against the lofty, striking, white figure of Querelle.' A moment after, 'the Armenian was kneeling on the cushions before him. The pale pink silk kimono, stitched with gold and silver birds, opened onto a torso and legs which were perfectly smooth and white'. Meanwhile, irreparable words have been uttered by the soon-to-be criminal. 'My name is Querelle, a sailor . . .' In telling him his identity, the thief is condemning his confidant to death. 'We cannot put it better than this,' Genet writes. 'He [Querelle] was as at ease in that room as in a mother's stomach. He was warm.'

With this glimpse of a primitive scene, the following one, the scene of the crime, is set up.

Joachim let his hand slide as high as the sailor's testicles. He began to stroke them as he murmured,

58 Ibid., p. 212.

'These treasures, these jewels . . .' Fiercely Querelle crushed his lips against the Armenian's mouth. He hugged him very tight in his powerful arms.

'Thou art a star immense and thy light will forever brighten my life. Thou art a golden star. Protect me forever . . .'

Querelle strangled him.

A little further on:

A little queer was something very soft. It died gently. Nothing got broken in the process.

And a little after:

If this were a typical queer—a creature so crushable, so soft and delicate, a thing so fragile, light and airy, so clear and transparent, a being so melodiously gifted with tender, honey-sweet words—then one was almost justified in killing it since it was made to be killed, in the same way as Venetian glass simply cries out to feel the weight of the fist of a horny-handed warrior who will smash it to smithereens without so much as a scratch being inflicted, unless by some mischance a sharp and glittering splinter insidiously, hypocritically, slits the skin and lodges deep within the flesh. If it was a queer, it was certainly not a man, and nowhere near a man's weight. It was something in the nature of a kitten, a fawn, a goldfinch, a blind-worm, or a dragonfly; something so provocatively and precisely exaggerated in its fragility that it must inevitably invite death. And what is more, it went by the name of Joachim.[59]

What is closer to a musical fantasy than this exorbitant whim? What could be more theatrical, more artificial, more contrived? What could be nearer to the circus, or further from the tragic universe of Dostoevsky?

'Never use adjectives your sentence could do without,' Genet had, in substance, said to me once when we were talking of writing. *When you have used an adjective, immediately take it out and see if the image misses it, if it really needs it, if it does not hold up better without it.* In his monologue, his painless elegy to the memory of the strangled Armenian, Genet uses eighteen adjectives . . . Which implies his crime 'needs' them here, that it is *performed*, the decoration, the face paint, the garland for a masked ball.

In fact, there is hardly a single executioner in Genet's works who is not connected to his victim by an umbilical cord. The person who dies is the child, or the double, of the one who kills, the object of a suicide as much as a murder: Jean, split in two. 'But to kill, to kill you, Jean,' he wrote in *Our Lady of the Flowers*, 'Wouldn't it be a question of knowing how I would behave as I watched you die by my hands?'[60] These lines contain the principal motive for

59 Ibid., pp. 214–19.

60 Genet, *Our Lady of the Flowers*, p. 120.

the crimes in Genet's works, as well as the reason he so strongly associates sexual—homosexual—fantasy with the act of murder. The death given and the death received create—body to body—the form of an incestuous couple melding together.

Redemption. Any meaning the word may have had for Genet came, naturally, from turning it on its head. To him, the crime compensates for the fault—the original sin—of birth. Once more, it is death that stirs life, revives it, gives it what it needs to *live*. He wrote:

> Without pretending, for example, that I want to be redeemed through it, though I do yearn for redemption. I would like to kill. As I have said above, rather than an old man, I would like to kill a handsome blond boy, so that, already united by the verbal link that joins the murderer and the murdered (each existing thanks to the other), I may be visited, during days and nights of hopeless melancholy, by a handsome ghost of which I would be the haunted castle.[61]

In his essay on the Karamazovs, Freud identified the Russian novelist's desire for redemption with these words: 'A criminal is to him [Dostoevsky] almost a Redeemer, who has taken on himself the guilt which must else have been borne by others.' It is disturbing, to say the least, to

61 Ibid.

think that for each of our examples—though for radically different reasons—the criminal ends up in the position of a 'saviour'. One can't help beginning to wonder—though it is going out on a limb—if the muzhiks, in killing his father, were not in a sense the authors of the crime which he, Dostoevsky, was *unable* to commit: 'redeemers', almost. Whereas perhaps Genet, lacking a father and muzhiks, granted the criminal he held so dear, so vital, the power to tear apart the screen of reality and to erect another against it: an all-powerful reality, mental rather than physical, steered, like a *waking* dream, with an iron will.

During his four years of prison camp, Dostoevsky took notes but did not otherwise write. His works would wait until after the end of his life as a convict, away from the crowded conditions he abhorred. For Genet it was the opposite. It is true that his prison was not a Siberian labour camp, far from it. Nonetheless, it was during his incarceration that the essence of his poetic work was conceived. 'I wrote in prison. Once I became free I was lost.'[62] In *The House of the Dead*, you survive or you die, you do not live. In *Our Lady of the Flowers* or *Miracle of the Rose*, the scent of death arouses desire and sustains life. Genet's prison is his mother; he says so in as many words.

> I endowed the colony with all these ridiculous and
> disturbing attributes of womankind, until there

62 Genet, *The Declared Enemy*, p. 239.

was established in my mind not the physical image of a woman but rather a soul-to-soul bond between us which exists only between mother and son and which my undeceivable soul recognized . . . Little by little the veils fell away from it. The mother materialized. In the cell, I really and truly returned to her throbbing breast and had real dialogues with her, and perhaps these transformations which made Mettray my mother added an incestuous feeling to my love for Divers, who had come from the same womb as I.[63]

At the end of his life, he added 'Prisons I found ratherly motherly—more so than the dangerous streets of Amsterdam, Paris, Berlin and Barcelona.'[64] Therefore, unlike the *House of the Dead*—which in Russian literally means 'the dead house'—Genet's prison is the living house. 'The criminal child,' he wrote, 'is one who has forced open a door to a forbidden place. He wants the door to open onto the most beautiful scene in the world: if he has warranted incarceration, he wants it to be brutal. Worthy, in the end, of the *pains he has taken* to defeat it.'[65]

This infernal paradise is everything at once: a haven for writing, a shelter for love affairs and the trench from which he could wage his war against the country that made him a bastard—France. Yet, during this period, this

63 Genet, *Miracle of the Rose*, p. 196.
64 Genet, *Prisoner of Love*, p. 172.
65 Genet, 'The Criminal Child' [our translation].

same France, or, rather, another France, was invaded by an enemy to be reckoned with: the Nazi army. How could Genet steer away from, laugh at or otherwise wriggle out of being saddled with such an inconvenient ally? At the risk of sounding biased, let us simply say that neither his genius nor his humour were always enough to get him out of trouble. Evil may go down well in a poem, but when Genet rubs shoulders with its embodiment, even just to get a laugh, he knocks his tightrope-walker to the ground before he begins to dance.

All the same, I shall try not to distort the picture at the point where a complicated story turns into a scandalous headline.

1944. Upon his definitive release from prison, which coincided, unfortunately for him, with the liberation of France, Genet organized and mobilized his troops: his selves multiplied. He became an army in himself. He sneered at the general jubilation and prepared his counterattack. In order to understand such an enterprise, we must imagine the stage as it was set in his own head. 'And what if I am free tomorrow?' he asked himself the day before his hearing. 'Free, in other words exiled among the living. I have made myself a soul to fit my dwelling. My cell is so sweet.'[66] In *Miracle of the Rose*, he went further, projecting this threat of liberation and separation onto the whole country, onto

---

66 Genet, *Our Lady of the Flowers*, p. 305 [translation modified].

occupied France itself. The seeds of *Funeral Rites* and *The Criminal Child* were already sown.

> I realize that I loved my colony with my flesh, just as it may be said that as the Germans were preparing to leave, France realized, in losing the rigidity they had imposed on her, that she had loved them. She squeezed her buttocks. She begged the supplanter to remain inside her. 'Stay a while,' she cried. Thus, Touraine was no longer fecundated.[67]

Why Touraine? Because 'of all the state prisons of France, Fontevrault is the most disquieting'.[68] Thus commences the hymn to Harcamone.

> I shall not try to define the essence of its power over us: whether this power be due to its past, its abbesses of royal blood, its aspect, its walls, its ivy, to the transient presence of convicts bound for the penal colony at Cayenne, to its prisoners, who are more vicious than those elsewhere, to its name— none of this matters. But to all these reasons was added, for me, another: that it was, during my stay at the Mettray Reformatory Colony, the sanctuary to which our childhood dreams aspired.[69]

Cut off from his sanctuary, Genet was cut off from the theatre of his fantasies, cut off from what he had called

---

67 Genet, *Miracle of the Rose*, p. 237 [translation modified].

68 Ibid., p. 5.

69 Ibid.

'this far-off universe I live in'.[70] His return to earth could only take on the appearance of a fall. How, then, would his shattered 'cell' renew and reconstitute itself on the stage of the world outside?

But first a word on the foundation of his political choices: 'I would like for the world not to change so that I can be against the world,' he said.[71] He could not have been clearer. Neither on the left or the right, he explained, but on the side of the 'lone man'. 'Lone' is all very well, but under what conditions and in relation to whom? That was where he had to invent, to improvise. Now, he was forced to adjust his answer to this question—which he had given firmly in favour of the murderer, rubbing his glory in the face of the *bien-pensants*—in response to the loss of prison's refuge. The transition from being nestled within the walls of this closed, maternal world to a world with an open horizon, where his enemy's face blurred and was lost in the crowd, required him to create a new language, a new definition of the 'lone man'. This definition, which took shape first among immigrant workers, then the Black Panthers, followed by the Red Army Faction and the Palestinians, sends us back, first and foremost, to the first kind of solitude Genet knew: his own. The form of solitude that he kept to himself. Due to pride, without question,

70 Ibid [our translation].

71 Genet, *The Declared Enemy*, p. 132.

but also and, most of all, for calculated, strategic reasons. He knew that relinquishing even an iota of it would have seriously undermined his plan of revenge and attack, which consisted of making himself inaccessible, systematically burning all bridges between himself and the upholders of order. In short, never being 'helpful', with one sort of exception: when it suited him and on his conditions. Along with, therefore, his redoubtable capacity for both persuasion and betrayal, without ever showing the shadow of a regret. The solitude Genet never spoke of, other than in the most neutral, bare, hermetic terms, was the solitude that stemmed from his birth.

He always defied any attempt to suppress his voice and always outdid any attempt to rival his brazenness and effrontery, yet he kept an almost religious silence, throughout his entire life, with regard to the starting point of his adventure: the shock of abandonment. Genet made brilliant use of this great silence, which grew and branched out beneath his feet like a root, splicing time exactly where he pleased. He used it so that the curtain would rise and fall on his authority alone and, in a sense, he used it to wrench the time of his origins out of historical time. To the extent that the theatrical *mise en scène* of his written *oeuvre* re-established itself in his political struggles, changing in appearance only. Fundamentally, the principle remained the same: control every aspect of the action and decide solely on his own terms the order of events, who would be under the spotlight when, and even what, the people he was supposed to be supporting would say. In other words, remove any notion of a 'beginning' from time. It is only starting from here, from deep within his theatre, that listening to his political voice makes sense. At the same time as we resign ourselves, once more—whether his words inspire joy or aversion in us—to regaining our seats as spectators. Because, in the end, he is the quintessential 'lone man'.

One thing is certain: twenty years after his death, he continues to fan the flames of burning controversies, pushing people into opposing camps, ensnaring good souls. In short, achieving his goal: chaos. And generally, it is not crossing the line that actually causes him to end up in the dock so often. It is crossing it with his hands in his pockets. Vice can be tolerated. It is his sly look, which he carried to the grave, that is deemed unacceptable. So many people find it easier to forgive an all-powerful army for utterly crushing a country than to forgive a lone man who spits in their face. Genet knew this, he played this card all the way, right to the limits of understanding. He knew that lack of guilt would always be the most effective of his weapons. He could count on it to make himself lastingly hated after he methodically cut his ties. In a sense, he was the anti-Raskolnikov, the anti-Stavrogin, the anti-Karamazov. He was doubtlessly sincere when he declared himself delighted that the 'French army had surrendered to the troops of an Austrian corporal', but to conclude, on that basis, as some do, that he would have supported the Nazi army, that he could in any way have identified with it, is an aberration, a fundamental error. Associating Genet with the Nazi project would be to deny and erase the foundation underlying his life and work: the use of the most radical of solitudes, given expression by any means possible, including violence, to fight against domination and the rule of might, order and the state, the unified masses, military parades and standing to attention. But we have arrived, through the narrowest of passages, at the subject which requires the most careful attention to accuracy. Once again, he has not made the task easy. Perhaps it is better that way. Under these conditions, the further I progress, the more this undertaking—thinking Genet—will, if all goes well, merge with the very act of thinking in itself.

What happens in *Funeral Rites*? Genet's ex-lover, Jean Decarnin, to whom the book is dedicated, is a young communist who dies on the barricades, just before the liberation of France. He is killed by a stray bullet from the gun of a member of the Milice, the Vichy militia to which Genet owed 'the delicate pleasure of seeing France terrorized by kids between sixteen and twenty'.[72] The nightmare is just beginning. 'The more Jean's soul inhabits me—the more Jean himself inhabits me—the fonder I shall be of

72 Genet, *Funeral Rites*, p. 78.

cowards, traitors and petty no-goods.'[73] The scenes succeed one another:

> I would like to be an out-and-out bastard and kill those I love, those handsome adolescents, so that through a great pain I can know the great depth of my love for them.[74]
>
> . . . Was it possible that in my personal life I was accepting without anguish one of those against whom Jean had fought to the death? For the quiet death of that twenty-year-old communist who, on 19 August 1944, was picked off at the barricades by the bullet of a charming young collaborator, a boy whose grace and age were his adornment, puts my life to shame.[75]

Further on, sorrow's delirium 'invents this blossoming':

> It was betrayal that was the hardest for me. However, I had the admirable courage to move further away from human beings by a greater fall, to turn my most tormented friend over to the police. I myself brought the detectives to the apartment in which he was hiding, and made a point of being paid off for my betrayal before his very eyes. Of course that betrayal causes me tremendous

73 Ibid., p. 98.

74 Genet, *Funeral Rites* [our translation].

75 Genet, *Funeral Rites*, p. 17.

suffering, which reveals to me my friendship for my victim and an even deeper love for man; but in the midst of that suffering it seemed to me, when shame had burned me through and through, that there remained amidst the flames or rather the fumes of shame a kind of imperishable diamond with sharp clean lines, rightly called a solitaire.[76]

Is this a slip of the tongue or a deliberate provocation? Sixty pages later, the metaphor of the *solitaire* ['loner'] returns as he describes someone else: 'Jewellers call a good-sized, well-cut diamond a solitaire. One speaks of its "water", that is, its limpidness. Which is also its brilliance. Hitler's solitude made him sparkle.'[77]

If there is one man who embodies the difference between shame and guilt, it is certainly Genet. More than the difference, the struggle, with the former invariably triumphing over the latter. His shame, it must be understood, does not answer to men but to a higher idea: to God or to gods. With them, as we have seen, Genet is not in enemy terrain, he can switch roles, he has leeway. Having left the judgement of men behind, his stain belongs to him alone, it is *pure*. He can display it, suffer from it, 'throw himself lower than the ground', offering no mercy to his image and above

76 Ibid., p. 80.
77 Ibid., p. 126.

all—in a supreme act of pride—none to his pride. His own executioner, he remains all-powerful. Once again, he represents an inversion of the Dostoevskian character, where shame gives rise to guilt and guilt gives rise to shame, deepening the rupture. With Genet there is nothing of the sort. Which is also why, unlike the author of *Demons*, he does not succeed in separating himself from his characters, in making them live after having brought them into existence, which is to say, after him. He was, in fact, the first to confirm this: 'my books are not novels,' he said to Sartre, 'because none of my characters take decisions for themselves.' Yet it is precisely with *Funeral Rites*, written on his release from prison, that his multiple selves progress from their orbital arrangement and blend. Deprived of his stand-in mother—'my good, my gentle friend, my cell! My sweet retreat, mine alone'[78]—Genet 'sheds his skin' and makes his move, so to speak: he eats dead Jean, he eats himself, as his dreams had whispered to him in *Our Lady of the Flowers*: 'bursting with emotion, I wanted to swallow myself by opening my mouth very wide and turning it over my head, so that it would take in my whole body, and then the universe, until all that would remain of me would be a ball of eaten stuff which little by little would be annihilated.'[79] And so the perilous novel was born: *Funeral Rites*, or the grim experiment of testing fantasy in the laboratory of reality.

---

78 Genet, *Our Lady of the Flowers*, p. 129.
79 Ibid., p. 75 [translation modified].

The cast: Jean Decarnin in his coffin; Erik, the soldier from Berlin in his mother's bed; Paulo, his brother, sleeping with Riton, the militiaman, then with Hitler as played by Genet; Pierrot, the informer, a petty killer, 'as bad as a militiaman'; and, finally, the Führer. Here is one of Genet's more successful descriptions of him: 'Could it be that a simple moustache made up of straight, black hairs, possibly dyed by L'Oréal, possessed the sense of: cruelty, despotism, violence, rage, froth, lies, strangulation, death, forced marches, parades, prisons, knives?'[80]

'But this bimbo's just a little old guy of fifty, after all,' Paulo thinks later, under the caresses of the 'Master of the World'.[81]

I was officiating simultaneously at a funeral and a wedding; I merged the symbolic encounter of the two processions into a single movement. And even from here, I was able, by fixing my gaze and remaining motionless, or almost, to delegate my powers to the famous actor in Nuremberg who was playing the role in which I was prompting him from my room or from my place beside Jean's coffin. He was strutting, he was gesticulating and roaring before a crowd of spellbound, raving Storm Troopers who were thrilled to feel that they were the necessary extras in a performance that

---

80 Genet, *Funeral Rites* [our translation].
81 Ibid., p. 136.

was taking place in the street . . . the sublime officiant was Hitler playing the role of Hitler. He was representing me.[82]

But who was Genet, putting on the boots of the German soldier, borrowing the soul of Riton the militiaman or trying on the moustache of that 'old queen', the Führer, representing? What imaginary territory was he defending? Did his new 'freedom', unfaithful to the freedom he had had as a convict, need to be accompanied—in order for him to save himself and poetry from it—by a damnation greater than that of prison, a new level of hatred for France, a reassertion of exile from the 'world of the living'? Whatever the case may be, there is a crucial point within this parody that it would be seriously wrong to trivialize: by making Hitler a 'faggot', Genet, whether or not he was aware of the existence of the camps, inflicted upon the Nazi monster the identity of those he had sent to be cremated, in their hundreds of thousands, in the gas ovens.

I hope my reader will forgive me for returning again to the leitmotif of the great absence—the invisible centre of the spider's web—but there is a 'memory' in the novel (in the form of a digression, left unfinished) which unavoidably brings us back to it: 'One day when I went to see Jean, hoping to spend the evening with him, I found him dressed up, with a tie, which was unusual for him, ready to go out.

82 Ibid., pp. 75–6.

My arrival seemed to vex him.' Genet orders Decarnin to give an account of his movements, but Decarnin promises his jealous lover that he is not going to see men but girls. Genet does not believe him and asks him to swear on it.

'You swore but you're going to go anyway, on the sly . . . '

'I told you I'm not.'

'You're going to go . . . '

'I'm telling you I won't. I said no, all right.'

'Swear it.'

'Yes.'

'Swear on your old man's grave.'

'Yes.'

'Say I swear.'

'Yes, I swear.'

'On your father's grave?'

'Yes.'

'Well say it. Say the words.'

He hesitated, then, under my stare he said:

'I swear it on my father's grave . . . '

I noticed right away that, consciously or not, he had mumbled the words 'my father's grave' very quickly, so that they were almost indistinct. My habits of thought and my trickery made me latch on to it. I will come back to it.[83]

83 Genet, *Funeral Rites* [our translation].

As with Smerdyakov, Genet did not say any more about it, did not come back to it. And for good reason. Of the two Jeans, the one who has light cast upon him through these words—*my father's grave*—is not Decarnin but Genet. Is it a coincidence that the author of the phrase 'I will always meet your slyness with my cunning'[84] finds the word 'trickery' applies to him more than 'cunning' in this instance? My own thoughts are that he suddenly felt himself under threat (from himself) of losing the most precious of his masks, the mask whose loss would *humanize* his entire project and therefore make it self-destruct. He immediately responded to his own dirty tricks with cunning, by falling silent.

My father's grave: a magnificent self-portrait of Genet's Fall.

Wrote Nietzsche:

> In the writings of a recluse . . . one always hears something of the echo of the wilderness, something of the murmuring tones and timid vigilance of solitude; in his strongest words, even in his cry itself, there sounds a new and more dangerous kind of silence, of concealment. He who has sat day and night, from year's end to year's end, alone with his soul in familiar discord and discourse, he who has become a cave-bear, or a treasure-seeker,

---

84 Genet, 'The Criminal Child' [our translation].

or a treasure-guardian and dragon in his cave—it
may be a labyrinth, but can also be a gold-mine—
his ideas themselves eventually acquire a twilight-
colour of their own, and an odour, as much of the
depth as of the mould, something uncommunica-
tive and repulsive, which blows chilly upon every
passer-by . . . Every philosophy also *conceals* a
philosophy; every opinion is also a lurking-place,
every word is also a mask.[85]

It is uncertain how far Genet, who extolled 'the
audacity of breaking with the world's omnipotence'[86] is a
descendant of Nietzsche, who said, 'I am not a man. I am
dynamite.'[87] We know he read the German's works pas-
sionately, right until the end of his life, but he left few
written traces of this reading. I am not seeking to elaborate
limited information, nor, of course, to undermine the
inimitable qualities of each of these very different writers,
but only to shed light on this portrait of Genet by com-
paring him with the wildest and most brilliant of his
predecessors, who, half a century before him, had waged
war on the established order of thought. What did they

85 Friedrich Nietzsche, *Beyond Good and Evil* (Helen Zimmerman trans.)
(New York: Macmillan, 1914); available at https://goo.gl/PRg46F (last
accessed on 30 October 2015), n.p.

86 Genet, 'The Criminal Child' [our translation].

87 Friedrich Nietzsche, *Ecce Homo* (Anthony M. Ludovici trans.) (New
York: Macmillan, 1911); available at https://goo.gl/4U79KQ (last accessed
on 29 October 2015).

have in common? Here is a quick summary: the same rejection of morality, the same inversion of values—of *good* and *evil*, of *truth* and *falsehood*—the same mockery, the same demolition of monotheistic religion in general and Christianity in particular, the same love for the Greeks and Dionysus, the same correlation of cruelty with celebration, the same cursed feeling of having been chosen, the same taste for satire and for rupture, the same stance towards the reader, the same resort to masks in order to unmask, and ultimately the same aspiration to the omnipotence of the solitary man, unmoved by the *democratic ideal*. 'In reality two negations are involved in my title Immoralist,' wrote Nietzsche, 'I first of all deny the type of man that has hitherto been regarded as the highest—the good, the kind, and the charitable; and I also deny that kind of morality which has become recognized and paramount as morality-in-itself—I speak of the morality of decadence, or, to use a still cruder term, Christian morality.'[88]

What could be closer to the role played by Genet than the incarnation of this idea in the form of the 'superman'?

> Zarathustra, as the first psychologist of the good man, is perforce the friend of the evil man. When a degenerate kind of man has succeeded to the highest rank among the human species, his

---

88 Ibid.

position must have been gained at the cost of the reverse type—at the cost of the strong man who is certain of life. When the gregarious animal stands in the glorious rays of the purest virtue, the exceptional man must be degraded to the rank of the evil. If falsehood insists at all costs on claiming the word 'truth' for its own particular standpoint, the really truthful man must be sought out among the despised. Zarathustra allows of no doubt here; he says that it was precisely the knowledge of the good, of the 'best', which inspired his absolute horror of men. And it was out of this feeling of repulsion that he grew the wings which allowed him to soar into remote futures. He does not conceal the fact that his type of man is one which is relatively superhuman—especially as opposed to the 'good' man, and that the good and the just would regard his superman as the devil.[89]

And finally, to complete the picture, this crowning provocation from *The Antichrist*: 'Must I add that, in the whole New Testament, there appears but a *solitary* figure worthy of honour? Pilate, the Roman viceroy.'[90]

Thus spoke Nietzsche, thus lived Genet.

---

89 Ibid.

90 Friedrich Nietzsche, *The Antichrist* (H. L. Mencken trans.) (New York: Alfred A. Knopf, 1918); available at http://goo.gl/UeLl1m (last accessed on 29 October 2015).

And yet, if we examine the image more closely, in what ways does it unravel and diverge, including over the question of morality? Why do these two thinkers, who seem so close, diverge? Beside the fact that Nietzsche's undertaking was on an incomparable scale, he had a stated project: oblivious to the madness that awaited him at the end of the road, he thought of destruction as a stepping stone, a stage in the process of construction. His aim was 'the affirmation of life' and with it the emergence of a 'new man', the triumph of the future on the ashes of the present. This was not at all the case with Genet, who had no interest in humanity's transformation. However ambitious his megalomania, it had, unlike Nietzsche's, no dreams for the future. His project, his 'positive' mission was to be, in and of himself, without distinguishing between ends and means, an example of how to break away from the order of men. A 'heroic' assault, at the heart of which pride and shame would stimulate each other, copulate and fecundate each other. Damnation and redemption are now one and the same; the dance is born from the force and impact of the fall. And to obtain and sustain that hybrid state of discipline and degradation, Genet played on the present, all the time. Contrary to Nietzsche, he only made use of the past and the future in order to arrest the moment, to hold it fast, to make it bear—cross and resurrection blended into one—the entirety of all time. The moral conscience, according to Genet, is solitude taken to the pinnacle of will and brilliance; solitude learning, the hard way, painfully, joyfully, to overturn the world. It is a force that never seeks to resolve or explain but, rather, to dissolve and destroy. In other words, to reverse the gesture of expulsion that produced it and with that same gesture take under its wing everything and everyone spat out and rejected by the world. This is why he continually groups criminals and victims together. They are linked by a shared identity: humanity's cast-offs. 'I want to mingle with these humiliated creatures which are always on their bellies,' he wrote in *The Thief's Journal*.[91] Such are Genet's ethics and loyalties, enabling him to indulge in betrayal and squalor, and, more fundamentally—safe from any acquaintance with the morality of power—to lend his voice to those who cannot speak.

'The revolt of the slaves in morals begins in the very principle of *ressentiment* becoming creative and giving birth to values,' wrote Nietzsche. 'While every aristocratic morality springs from a triumphant affirmation of its own demands, the slave morality says "no" from the very outset to what is "out-side itself," "different from itself," and "not itself": and this "no" is its creative deed.'[92]

91 Jean Genet, *The Thief's Journal* (Bernard Frechtman trans.) (New York: Grove Press, 1987), p. 45.

92 Friedrich Nietzsche, *The Genealogy of Morals* (Horace B. Samuel trans.) (New York: Boni and Liveright, 1910); available at: https://goo.gl/-Mke8xw (last accessed on 29 October 2015) [translation modified].

The author of *Beyond Good and Evil* (1886), whose 'fertile dualism' Lou Salomé so rightly emphasized, did not make a choice, at least never a final one. In every way and on all fronts, he is always torn between two directions: between 'aristocratic morality' and the 'morality of *ressentiment*'. His paradoxical love of balance continually sabotaged any victory one might have had over the other, eroding the powers of 'conviction' until they were worn out. The 'decisive mark of the higher nature,' he wrote, is 'to be in that sense self-contradictory, and to be actually still a battleground for those two opposites.'[93] The French poet, contrary to the German, swapped the concept of the stepping stone and transition for the concept of intransigence. 'As for me, I made my choice: I would side with crime,' he wrote in 'The Criminal Child'.[94] Not that we are obliged to take his word for it, but he does adopt, as with the fundaments of French grammar, a stubborn resistance to being pulled in different directions, impervious to the torments of indecision or contradiction. He is pro-violence and anti-order, on the side of both the 'slave's revolt' and the 'man of *ressentiment*', except that—and this is an important nuance—unlike the latter, he does not translate his fight against the enemy into a fight for 'good'. He is, in short, a unsatisfactory recruit, a 'man of *ressentiment*' who is too protective of his solitude not to betray his cause.

93 Ibid.
94 Genet, 'The Criminal Child' [our translation].

A poet. Nietzsche said 'everywhere that slave-morality gains the ascendancy, language shows a tendency to approximate the significations of the words "good" and "stupid"'.[95] Genet safely preserved himself from that 'stupidity'—his bad faith simultaneously served as a shield against 'goodness' and as fuel for his poetry.

In his book on Nietzsche, Ernst Bertram irrefutably shows how his anti-Christian passion and his crusade against Luther cannot be divorced from his attachment to, and loving hatred of, his religious roots: 'In searching for and demanding a "yea-saying, yea-doing" ideal for life, one that is truly vital, with all the intensity and all the unapologet-ically biased injustice of Luther, his Upper-Saxon compa-triot, Nietzsche is drawing on the same Lutheran, northern Protestant heritage as Goethe does in the first part of *Faust*.'[96]

For Genet, things were admittedly different, in the sense that, unlike Nietzsche, he was cut off from any filiation, any genealogy. Yet he too received a highly religious edu-cation in childhood, and not only would the Church be his most consistent and fertile source of metaphors but it also provided, in the Trinity, a very powerful way for him to

95 Nietzsche, *Beyond Good and Evil*, n.p.

96 Ernst Bertram, *Nietzsche: Attempt at a Mythology* (Robert E. Norton trans.) (Chicago: University of Illinois Press, 2009), p. 49.

transpose his orphaned birth. The Pietà and the Turin Shroud reversed become alternative images of himself. His 'self-invention' would be the fruit of another alliance, one no less strange: the language of the *Genius of Christianity* in the service of the *Antichrist*.

At Mettray we went to the toilet as follows: the shit-house was in the yard, behind each family dormitory. At noon and at six, on the way back from the shops, we would march in line, led by the elder brother, and stop in front of the four urinals. We would leave the line in fours to take a leak or pretend to. At the left were the latrines, which were four or five steps high so that the crap can was on a level with the ground. Each boy stepped from the line and went to one or the other, depending on the need he felt. He would let his belt hang from the door to show that the place was occupied. There was never any paper. For three years I wiped myself with my forefinger and the wall whitewashed my finger.

Miracle of the Rose[97]

1979. He was living in the Pigalle neighbourhood. A new building, ordinary, designed like a hotel, with several flats on each floor. His bedroom was virtually bare. I remember a window, a mattress on the floor and several

97 Genet, *Miracle of the Rose*, p. 170.

drawings by his friend Jacky, up on the wall. On the beige, newly laid carpet was the still life comprising his portable little cemetery: cigarette packets, metal lids serving as ashtrays, ossuaries of cigarette butts.

By the front door, a bathroom and inside it, behind a door, the toilet.

He was struggling to swallow. I brought him soup several times. He seemed pleased to see me, asking me lots of questions about the war in Lebanon and about the Palestinians and also talking to me of music and books, though never of his own. 'How is your Romanian right-winger doing?' he asked me one day. He meant Cioran. We laughed. 'You have to admit that he's a great writer, all the same!' I shot back. After a lengthy smile savoured in silence, he ended up saying 'yes' (the curt, magnanimous little 'yes' of a prison guard). That same day or one like it—I cannot remember—Genet flew into an uncontrollable rage. As I was on the point of leaving, I got out a large bin liner I had brought with me in order to clear the place up, without telling him—I thought I was being helpful!—dozens of empty milk bottles stacked against the wall in the WC. Genet, lying in his room, heard the noise. He jumped up and yelled, 'Don't touch them, put all those bottles back.' He was beside himself. It was only many years later that I understood the intimate, holy, sacrosanct link between this white, fetid-smelling liquid—sour milk remains, possessively kept in the toilet—and sperm, as well as the 'sour milk' of his origins.

Milk seemed to pursue Genet: in the Morvan, the region of his childhood, famous for its wet-nurses and their establishments, known as 'dairies', and in his adoptive family, with the Régnier's milking cow, which he would take out to graze, a book in his hand . . . As for the little kingdom of the WC, no one has said more about it than him, or said it better.

'The peace I used to seek in the outhouse,' he wrote in Our Lady of the Flowers,

> the one I am going to seek in the memory of it, is a reassuring and soothing peace . . . I would remain for hours squatting in my cell, roosting on my wooden seat, my body and soul prey to the odour and darkness; I would feel mysteriously moved, because it was there that the most secret part of human beings came to reveal itself, as in a confessional. Empty confessionals had the same sweetness for me.[98]

Or again:

> The smell rising from the blocked latrines, over-flowing with shit and yellow water, stir childhood memories which rise up like a black soil mined by moles . . . a whole life which I thought subter-ranean and forever buried rises to the surface, to the air, to the sad sun, which give it a smell of decay, in which I delight.[99]

98 Genet, Our Lady of the Flowers, pp. 98–9.
99 Ibid., p. 97.

I hope the reader will believe me: I have just—with the lines above barely written—had a telephone conversation with Albert Dichy.[100] Here it is:

My question came first:

'The idea that Genet's father was a foreigner was pure fantasy, wasn't it?'

'Yes, it was a fantasy.'

'We still don't know anything about his father?'

'In fact we do, the archives of the Assistance publique have now allowed access to the relevant file.'

'So? Do we know the name?'

'Indeed . . . Genet's father's name was Blanc.'

Failing to hide my emotion, I asked another question:

'Is it possible that Genet knew?'

'It seems highly unlikely.'

Blanc. White . . . The skin colour Genet spent his whole life waging war against. White, his round head, which he sent rolling among the blacks and the Palestinians— 'what did they want this white head, with its white skin, white hair, white unshaven beard—this white, pink, round head forever in their midst.'[101] White, his memory of himself, 'a

---

100 Albert Dichy is the co-author, with Pascal Fouché, of a biography of Genet. He is also the literary director of IMEC, the contemporary publishing archive and director of the Fonds Genet.

101 Genet, *Prisoner of Love*, p. 96 [translation modified].

child too white, like half-baked bread',[102] white, the little boy reminding him of his childhood, 'in the white skirts' of his mother, white, the paradise of the infirmary: 'It loomed out of our daily fatigue like a cool resting-place because of its whiteness: glaze of the coifs, of the aprons, the smocks, the sheets, the bread, the mashed vegetables, the porcelains. We sometimes felt like burying ourselves in that glaze, in that snow.'[103]

White, 'the white gentleman who was judging two blacks',[104] white, 'for two thousand years God has been white,' says the missionary in *The Blacks*, 'He eats on a white tablecloth. He wipes his white mouth with a white napkin. He picks at white meat with a white fork. (A pause.) He watches the snow fall.'[105]

White like Snow, the negress, who interrupts the court's long sobbing, 'then let me tell you now—all of you—I've been burning for so long, burning with such ardent hatred, that I'm a heap of ashes,' and who later cries, 'Wondrous, indeed, the malady that makes you ever whiter and that leads you to ultimate whiteness.' Then, bursting out laughing, she says, 'But what's that I see flowing down your black stockings? So it was true, Lord Jesus, that behind the mask of a cornered white is a poor

---

102 Genet, *Our Lady of the Flowers* [our translation].

103 Genet, *Miracle of the Rose*, p. 230.

104 Genet, *The Declared Enemy*, p. 61 [translation modified].

105 Genet, *The Blacks*, p. 24.

trembling Negro?'[106] White, the voice of Divine, after
Harcamone's death, 'his white voice which I imagined as
a film star's voice, an image-voice, a flat voice . . .',[107] white,
the wilted daisy of the little maid in *Funeral Rites*, white,
'soft' Divine wishing for the embrace of 'a stone man with
hard angles' white, the head of the executed man in its basket, the Rose of the Winds compass motif carved into the
plaster, and the corpse of Sonia, under the eye of black
Clément, 'the death of a white threw him, the death of a
black would have been less troubling',[108] white, the hand of
Our Lady, the ceramic latrine where Mignon, trousers down
. . . 'the swan, borne up by its mass of white feathers'[109] and
Harcamone in chains, going to the scaffold: 'but the fervour of our admiration and the burden of saintliness
which weighed on the chain that gripped his wrists . . .
caused the chain to be transformed before our unaston-
ished eyes into a garland of white flowers.'[110]

And Félicité, the black, confronting the white queen:

To you, black was the colour of priests and under-
takers and orphans. But everything is changing.
Whatever is gentle and kind and good and tender
will be black. Milk will be black, sugar, rice, the

---

106 Ibid., pp. 17, 57–8.

107 Genet, *Our Lady of the Flowers* [our translation].

108 Genet, *The Blacks* [our translation].

109 Genet, *Our Lady of the Flowers*, p. 26.

110 Genet, *Miracle of the Rose*, p. 17.

sky, doves, hope, will be black. So will the opera
to which we shall go, blacks that we are, in black
Rolls Royces to hail black kings, to hear brass
bands beneath chandeliers of black crystal.[111]

And the words at the end in Snow's mouth: 'the stair-
way to death is interminable. And bright as day. Pale.
White. Infernal.'[112] And whiter than white, the dazzling
reflection of light in a landscape drawn by the artist
with hard pencil—'it is white—the white page—which
Giacometti seems to have chiselled'.[113] And it is again from
white that the first page of *Prisoner of Love* comes forth:

> The page that was blank to begin with is now
> crossed from top to bottom with tiny black
> characters—letters, words, commas, exclamation
> marks—and it's because of them the page is said
> to be legible. But a kind of uneasiness, a feeling
> close to nausea, an irresolution that stays my
> hand—these make me wonder: do these black
> marks add up to reality? The white of the paper
> is an artifice that's replaced the translucency
> of parchment and the ochre surface of clay
> tablets; but the ochre and the translucency and the

111 Genet, *The Blacks*, p. 106.

112 Ibid., p. 124.

113 Jean Genet, 'The Studio of Alberto Giacometti' [our translation].
Available in *Selected Writings* (Edmund White ed. and introd.) (New
York: Harper Perennial, 1995), pp. 309–39.

whiteness may all possess more reality than the signs that mar them.[114]

And right at the end of this last work, Jean, the bastard son of Camille Genet and Monsieur Blanc, seals the inseparable destiny of yellow and white.[115] 'Inseparable', apart from in the astonishing digression provoked by a fried egg—the work of a painter as much as of a writer—where the 'white' occurs eight times, while the yellow occupies the centre without ever being mentioned:

> If you want the white of a fried egg to look good you have to break the egg into some already hot butter. Then the white quickly loses its transparency and viscosity and turns into a kind of white enamel with a thin dark edge. That's when the egg should be served. If the egg is fresh the colour is usually somewhere between off-white and ivory. This is not due to it alone partly to the proximity of another enamel that's closer to green or sometimes red, but usually green. This second enamel also looks rather swollen. The Charles II cross worn by the Spanish ambassador similarly consisted of a round of green enamel surrounded by a band of white enamel. Later, in Amman in August 1972, I saw a harder white on the chest of the French ambassador—on the cross worn by a

114 Genet, *Prisoner of Love*, p. 5.
115 Referring to the yellow flowers of the broom (*genet*). [Trans]

Chevalier of the Legion of Honour. The military attaché was wearing the medal of the Resistance. I noticed that the fineness of an enamel, whatever its colour, resided in two details: a slight swelling, subsiding near the edges, and a fine, almost invisible network of tiny cracks, probably due to the firing. If you examine a gob of spit through a magnifying glass you discover much the same complex mystery as you can detect with the naked eye in a Chardin or a Vermeer . . . [116]

Last but not least, 'chance' had it that, seven years after his death, Jean Genet's biographer should be named Edmund . . . White.

When Leïla Shahid expressed concern about Genet's physical exhaustion during the correction of the proofs of *Prisoner of Love*, Genet replied, solemnly, 'I am putting the white spaces between the paragraphs.' In the days leading up to his death he was still at it. These 'white spaces' were not simply employed to space out the text, far from it: they had a vital role, they were part of the writing as much as the words were. You only have to look at the text with this in mind to understand it. Each of these seemingly innocent empty spaces is calculated. Sometimes it is a silence made to last, sometimes the opposite: a silence that prepares the

---

116 Genet, *Prisoner of Love*, p. 419 [translation modified].

arrival of noise, of fracture. Some of them are holes, death-traps, others are bridges. There are transparent, translucent ones, and others thick and impenetrable. There are large white spaces, equal to five or seven lines, and, more frequently, medium and small ones. In some of them, years, centuries, flow by. In others, mere seconds. Some have the power to bind together the paragraphs they separate, others bury or incinerate the words as if to emphasize the strength or the pallor of those that follow on. Genet did everything with white. He treated it as a site of death and of birth, as a marker of space and time, as a mask, as a mirror.

'When a drawing has too many mistakes in it . . . ,' he wrote, 'an artist rubs it out. Two or three rubs with the eraser and the paper's blank again. With France and Europe rubbed out I was faced with a blank of liberty that was to be filled with Palestine as I experienced it, but with touchings-up that worry me.'[117]

With these 'touchings-up'—a move away from revolution in the direction of law and order—signs of a new separation emerge, a new whiteness to come. Genet—who directed everything—never stopped giving reality theatrical roles which it could only end up betraying once the play was finished.

117 Ibid., p. 428.

Carte blanche. In July 1948, when Genet was again threatened with prison for past robberies, Sartre and Cocteau enlisted the help of other artists and intellectuals to successfully petition for him to be spared. The following month, he wrote a text of rare violence for a French radio programme, *Carte Blanche*. It was at first accepted, but then rejected by the producers. The title was 'The Criminal Child'. 'Saint-Maurice, Saint-Hilaire, Belle-Isle, Eysse, Aniane, Montesson and Mettray are names which may mean nothing to you. In the head of every child who has just committed a crime, whether serious or petty, these names are the sound, for a fixed period, of their fate.'[118]

This 'fixed period' which Genet held up as a threat was also his own, or, rather, the time he was in danger of losing and wanted to seize back at any cost. The cost would be exorbitant. It would primarily take the form of one delirious page, where the former convict disputed the attention given to the gas ovens and the concentration camps, arguing that it overshadowed that given to the 'children's prisons'. This is the page in question:

118 Genet, 'The Criminal Child' [our translation].

The newspapers are still showing photographs of corpses spilling out of silos or strewn over the plains, caught in barbed wire and in the crematory ovens. They show the torn-out fingernails and the tattooed skin, tanned into lampshades: Hitler's crimes. But no one is paying attention to the children's detention camps and the prisons of France, where, since time immemorial, torturers have been persecuting children and men. It is irrelevant whether some are innocent and others guilty in the eyes of justice, whether supernatural or merely human. In the eyes of the Germans the French were guilty. Our cowardly treatment in prison is so bad that I envy your torture. Because it is the same as ours, better even. Heat helped the plant to grow. Since it was planted by the bourgeois who built the prisons of stone, with guards for both body and spirit, I rejoice to see the sower ravaged at last. Those fine people, who remain today as names gilded in marble, applauded when we were handcuffed and struck in the ribs by a cop. One snap of the fingers from one of their gendarmes was fed by the boiling blood of the heroes of the North; it grew to become a plant of wondrous beauty, tact and skill, a rose whose twisted petals, peeled back, revealing red and pink under a hellish sun, take on terrible names: Majdenek, Belsen, Auschwitz, Mauthausen, Dora. I take my hat off.[119]

How and why did Jean Genet come to write such an odious text, and stand by it without wavering? Two phrases in particular make the whole impossible to swallow: 'No one is paying attention' and 'I take my hat off' (even if, as Dichy pointed out to me, *I take my hat off* does not necessarily mean *well done*, in the context, but *I bow down in the face of this overwhelming horror*). What is striking, in any case, is the analogous exploitation of the names of the prisons and the names of the camps: 'Saint-Maurice, Saint-Hilaire, Belle-Isle, Eysse . . . Majdenek, Belsen, Auschwitz, Mauthausen . . . ' There is a blatant search for correspondence in the way he brings them together and plays them against one another. Genet is jealous and therefore childish and cruel, he knows and does not want to know that his experience of prison is 'surpassed', wiped out, by the terrible superiority of the Nazi hell. He is unyieldingly attached to writing that melds beauty and horror. This is the birth, thirty-six years apart, of two twin metaphors in his writing, or metaphors close enough to be twins, one regarding the concentration camps, the other about the massacres of Sabra and Shatila. This connection, which, as far as I am aware, has not previously been picked up on, also leads us to the knowledge that in using the metaphor

119 Ibid. [our translation].

of a rose to describe the Holocaust Genet in no way diminishes its terror and atrocity. Death was always presided over by a rose in his work. 'It was indeed roses that I had wanted,' he wrote, on Dercanin's funeral, 'for their petals are sensitive enough to register every sorrow and then convey them to the corpse, which is aware of everything.'[120]

Here are the two images:

> A rose whose twisted petals, peeled back, revealing red and pink under a hellish sun, take on terrible names: Majdenek, Belsen . . .

> I felt like I was at the centre of a compass [*une rose des vents*] whose every radius pointed to hundreds of dead.[121]

It nonetheless remains that in no other of his works is Genet as aggressive, as violent, towards his readers as in 'The Criminal Child'. These readers included, crucially, Cocteau and Sartre. Never did Genet have them so firmly in his sights, never did he have his heart more set on turning them against him. Be warned, is his underlying message for them—and for us: 'Acquitted for acting without discernment . . . the young criminal immediately refuses the indulgent understanding and concern of a society which he has just revolted against by committing his first crime.'[122]

---

120 Genet, *Funeral Rites*, p. 25.
121 Genet, *The Declared Enemy*, p. 211 [translation modified].
122 Genet, 'The Criminal Child' [our translation].

It is impossible not to think of the autobiographical quality of these words, written so shortly after his own acquittal. One also cannot help but think of those who, in his eyes, embodied 'indulgent understanding' and the worst of threats: 'concern'. Remember that two years earlier, in 1946, Genet had dedicated *The Thief's Journal* to Sartre and De Beauvoir.

> I have laid my finger, heavily and many times, on poverty and punished crime. It is towards these I shall go. Not with the premeditated intention of finding them, in the manner of Catholic saints, but slowly, without trying to evade the fatigues and horrors of the venture. But am I being clear? It is not a matter of applying a philosophy of unhappiness. Quite the contrary. The prison—let us name that place in both the world and the mind—towards which I go offers me more joys than your honours and festivals. Nevertheless, it is these which I shall seek. I aspire to your recognition, your consecration. Heroized, my book, which has become my Genesis, contains—should contain—the commandments which I cannot transgress. If I am worthy of it, it will reserve for me the infamous glory of which it is the great master, for to what shall I refer if not to it?[123]

123 Genet, *The Thief's Journal*, p. 268.

I see this epilogue as a farewell lament that has been undermined, eaten away by the impurity of the farewell, the incompleteness of the rupture. It is, in my opinion, one of the saddest, most solitary moments in Genet's work. Which does not mean that his words have no meaning for his future: 'my book, which has become my Genesis, contains—should contain—the commandments which I cannot transgress.' Not Christ, not the Pietà, not the 'Catholic saints', but Genesis . . . the signs of a comparison with the Jewish people are apparent. In addition, at the same time as *Les Temps Modernes* was publishing extracts from the book, Sartre published *Anti-Semite and Jew* (1946). This work, which proposed a rather uniform and reductive version of anti-Semitism on the one hand and of Jews on the other, could only irritate Genet. He had a conflicted relationship with Judaism, marked, as I will discuss further, by a strong animosity towards the idea of 'the chosen' and could get no satisfaction from a book which not only failed to use the word Judaism once but also settled for an essentialist approach, divorced from history. Which left his particular position out of it. If Genet ever had any anti-Semitic instincts, they in no way resembled the 'thought process' Sartre describes in his book. So much so that Genet—the pariah par excellence, but always of his own volition—this time found himself, without his consent, outlawed from a world where horror and compassion took place without him. This occurred at the same time as the simultaneous decline of his poetic drive and as his misfortune, temporarily derailing the subtle mechanism of his genius and his perversion, as in *Funeral Rites*.

However, this is probably the moment for a digression on the memories I retain of Genet's words on Judaism, with the caveat, of course, that these memories are limited in more than one respect: limited to a particular period—the end of the 1970s—and limited by the fact that our relationship was asymmetrical, to say the least. Even if he was always very careful never to crush his interlocutor with his knowledge, showing him or her all the more respect if they found it difficult to speak up and make themselves heard (many others have also mentioned this about him). I will begin with a fact I do not consider insignificant: I never heard a single anti-Semitic cliché from his lips, not a single violent or disdainful word towards a Jew for being Jewish. On the other hand, what is relevant to the issue in question is a subject he brought up more than once: 'the unacceptable idea of the chosen', as I mentioned a moment ago. I cannot remember his exact words, but here, without quotation marks, is a summary: *As soon as a people considers itself chosen, believes itself chosen, it sees itself as superior, different, above other men. I do not see any reason why this must be accepted. Why should a people be 'chosen' and superior?* This, essentially, was Genet's central take on the question, the refrain he returned to. One basic interpretation, which has already been put forward by others, comes back to the theme of rivalry. Rivalry over the idea of being 'chosen', because Genet himself lived like a 'chosen' and 'superior' being and—in an even more 'vital' sense—rivalry over unhappiness, over the 'exceptional' quality of his solitude. 'The Criminal Child' bears witness to this. Which is not to say that the question Genet asks can be dealt with summarily. It touches on the most complicated and elusive aspect of Jewish identity. Jewish thinkers, from Spinoza to Marx, Freud, Arendt, Adorno, Leo Strauss, Scholem, Levinas and many others have endlessly developed incredibly diverse and even directly contradictory interpretations. We know, for example, that for the first five writers mentioned the notion of a 'chosen people' is a myth and in no respect a reality. We also know that for the other three it is endowed with great significance, though it does not follow that this necessarily equates the notion of 'chosen' with that of superiority. I have no desire to enter into the exegesis of a debate whose nuances are beyond me, at least at present, but neither do I wish to leave the subject as taboo, nor skim over a question which, left unaddressed, will on the one hand encourage wild speculation and on the other impede avenues of thought. And as for these avenues of thought, if there is one thinker who opened and explored them unreservedly and who can therefore help us to understand Genet's position, it is Freud. 'Originally a Father religion [as Judaism], Christianity became a Son religion,' he wrote at the end of his study on Moses and monotheistic religion. 'I venture to assert,' he added, 'that the jealousy which the Jews evoked in the other peoples by maintaining that they were the first-born, favourite child of God the Father has not yet been overcome by those others, just as if the latter had given credence to the assumption.'[124]

Those last words—*as if the latter had given credence to the assumption*—shed more light on Genet's hostility towards Judaism than a thousand essays could. Sartre does not even take this hostility into account in *Anti-Semite and Jew*. Genet was among those who gave 'credence to the assumption', to the father's preference for the eldest son, the Jew. Or, rather, he was among those who gave 'credence' to idea that the son was asserting that preference and therefore claiming the right to live as 'superior' to other men. When one knows of Genet's rejection—his rejection by, and of, the father—one knows, to say the least, how intolerable an idea this would have been for him.

'The people, happy in their conviction of possessing truth, overcome by the consciousness of being the chosen, came to value highly all intellectual and ethical achievements. I shall also show how their sad fate, and the disappointments reality had in store for them, was able to strengthen all these tendencies.'[125] Freud's view of the question here is very close to Genet's. Freud, however, a Jew and an atheist,

---

124 Sigmund Freud, *Moses and Monotheism* (Katherine Jones trans.) (New York: Hogarth Press, 1939); available at https://goo.gl/tsjmaV (last accessed on 31 October 2015).

125 Ibid.

saw no glory or threat but only a subject for analysis and reflection, while Genet saw certain proof of an ancestral pride which not only competed with his own but also took a form he found arrogant and impenetrable and therefore intolerable: a 'closed circle'. Which perhaps offers the beginning of an explanation for a little remark he made, quoted by Sartre: 'When cornered, he [Genet] declares that he "couldn't go to bed with a Jew".'[126] In reality, Genet's feelings towards the Jewish people, associated in his mind with the elite, were comparable in more than one way with those the 'nobility' provoked in him. A passage from *Our Lady of the Flowers* points us in this direction. It recounts the moment when the murderer's fate is sealed: Our Lady of the Flowers is lost, headed for the guillotine.

> Overnight, the name of Our Lady of the Flowers was known throughout France, and France is used to confusion. Those who merely skim the news-papers did not linger over Our Lady of the Flow-ers. Those who go all the way to the end of the articles, scenting the unusual and tracking it down every time, brought to light a miraculous haul; these readers were schoolchildren and old women who, out in the provinces, have remained like Ernestine, who was born old, like Jewish children who at the age of four have the faces and gestures they will have at fifty.[127]

126 Sartre, *Saint Genet*, p. 203 [translation modified].
127 Genet, *Our Lady of the Flowers*, p. 266.

The last line of this passage has often been cited as clear proof of Genet's anti-Semitism. In my view, this is a superficial reading. Many Arabs, many Palestinians especially, have given me a similar impression: marked by history, they start wearing their adult face in childhood. I do not really see any offence here. I see, instead, a good opportunity, while we are on the subject, to remind ourselves of the literal meaning of the word Semite. But beyond these different interpretations, the question the text sets us is 'why Ernestine?' The missing piece of the puzzle is found seventy pages before. 'Ernestine's maiden name was Picquigny. No doubt about it, she was noble.' And her story, Genet tells us, is in the book. 'Ernestine's father had known the book. The same miracle had opened it at the same place and had shown him the name.'[128] But how, exactly, did Genet perceive the world of the aristocracy?

> Nobility is glamorous. The most equalitarian of men, though he may not care to admit it, experiences this glamour and submits to it. There are two possible attitudes towards it: humility or arrogance, both of which are explicit recognition of its power. Titles are sacred. The sacred surrounds and enslaves us. It is the submission of flesh to flesh. The Church is sacred. Its slow rites, weighed down with gold like Spanish galleons, ancient in meaning, remote from spirituality, give it an

128 Ibid., p. 195.

empire as earthly as that of beauty and that of
nobility. Culafroy of the light body, unable to
escape this potency, abandoned himself to it
voluptuously, as he would have done to Art had he
known it. The nobility has names as heavy and
strange as the names of snakes (already as difficult
as the names of lost divinities), strange as signs
and escutcheons or venerated animals, totems of
old families, war cries, titles, furs, enamels—
escutcheons that closed the family with a secret,
as a signet seals a parchment, an epitaph, a tomb.[129]

Once again, the key is in the text which, in this specific
case, is not without its projections and stereotypes. One
thing is certain: in Genet's eyes, the children of the aristocracy and those of Judaism shared the trait of being born
old. Ernestine, like the Jews, is a child of History and the
Book, the descendant of a long line whose future is drawn
from her past and who therefore has 'at the age of four the
face she will have at fifty'. This is the way Genet—
descended from nobody—displays his refusal to submit to
the prestige of the 'ancients', to the 'explicit recognition
of their power', to the 'sacred'. His rejection of 'heirs' is
closely tied up with his rejection of Law and, therefore, of
the Father. The fact remains, in the end, that the predom-
inant sentiment in his text is not hatred but fascination.
When all is said and done, one even begins to wonder if

129 Ibid., p. 194.

Jean Genet was not more attached to the *Ancien Régime* than the Revolution. He was even, perhaps, more of a rebellious son of the former, than an heir apparent of the latter. In short, what certain critics do not want to see as they hurry to sum everything up in one word—anti-Semitism—is that Genet harboured infinitely more hos-tility and contempt towards the 'bourgeoisie' than towards the 'nobility' or the 'Jews'. He undeniably had some anti-Semitic impulses and he did not refrain from inflicting them on the reader, with that precious malice he wielded so effectively, but did this really make him a genuine anti-Semite? If he had been, I cannot think of any inhibitions that would have prevented him from declaring it loud and clear. In any case, to speak of 'taboo' or 'truths too shameful to confess' in relation to the man for whom 'confessing' was an unparalleled way of challenging all convention and propriety seems as ridiculous to me as sending an army to attack an empty battlefield.

Yet we know that the 'targeted' critiques of Genet over the years have been, for the most part, connected with the Palestinian question and they often have one goal: to use his intervention to discredit the cause that he spent the last twenty years of his life fighting for. Again, it is hard to see the logic in thinking that the injustice visited upon a people could be refuted or in any way diminished by the—openly—subjective, fantasy-prone character of one of its sworn opponents.

'I have died many times over,' Genet once said to me as we were walking together. As I write this, I have the feeling that he may have shown us a different face for each of the lives he lived, death after death. And if one book stands out as a summation of his books, or, more precisely, as their metamorphosis—with cracks, joins, seams, appearances and disappearances, illuminations and darkness—it must be the last: *Prisoner of Love*. In the manner of a tapestry, the text weaves a collection of extremes so distant from one another that only the tightest of stitching—excessively tight—could ultimately succeed in filling the great gaps, making the thousand and one connections between the minuscule and the monumental, the minor incidents and the historic events, the satire and the poetry, the palaces, the slums and the deserts and, at the same time—stitch after stitch—the connection between one fedayeen and another, between the solitary man and the world, between Jean Genet and Jean Genet. Yet is precisely his place in all this, his relationship to himself, at the heart of the work, which is so remarkable here, and causes such difficulty. Although his place is central, as it is in the novels of his youth, the centre in question is no longer at the centre. It has *sunk*, the way the sun sinks below the horizon at sunset. Or, to reverse Pascal's words, from him are born and die circumferences whose vanished core is nowhere. In this final book, Genet's 'I's continually eclipse one another. They try out temporary identities, repeat former gestures, deliberately efface them, begin them again while changing their meaning, oscillate between existing and bringing into existence, between living again and dying, between loving imprisonment and solitary desertion. Of all Genet's works, this is perhaps the most arduous, the most complicated, the most perilous. Personally, I have read and reread it, each time—from one page, even from one phrase, to the next—with the contradictory feeling of being first enlightened and dazzled, then blinded and exasperated by the arrangement of the words and by the swirl of different currents: here calm, there raging; here limpid and transparent, there abrupt, or endlessly contorted; here fluid, there bombastic; first precious, affected and pompous, then sublime. Rarely has a book made me set my thoughts against him as much as with and for him. Which shows that Genet put the whole of himself into it. A Lebanese friend told me that while reading it, she caught herself looking for something other than words on the page. 'I dropped the book, angry at Genet for having put me in this crazy state,' she added, 'it was as if reading no longer counted, or, rather, as if reading forced one to stop reading and to see instead.' It is safe to surmise that he would have liked that.

If Jean Genet made his final home among the Palestinian fighters in Jordan, it was because this home had no more material reality, no more solid borders, than the moving shadow of a cloud or a 'makeshift forest, with any old leaves'.[130]

---

130 Genet, *Prisoner of Love*, p. 113.

Because not only was the world of the fedayeen *alone in the world*—a territory without a territory like a card game without cards—but it also was beyond the law, beyond time, freed from the need to endure: 'they brushed against death every day, every night'.[131] Although there was always the possibility of things going awry, the threat that this world might actually come into being in the shape of nation—'in which case I will no longer be there,' said Genet—for the moment there was only the moment, the ideal framework for all metamorphoses. From such a vantage point, the author of *Miracle of the Rose* could freely invent his death as one invents one's life, let himself be troubled, be the absence of trouble, and calmly declare: 'you could say that before he died a fedayee was light on the earth.'[132]

'I was a galley packed with stampeding males,' he wrote at the age of thirty-two.[133] Forty years on, his self-portrait has absorbed the beast and the galley. It is what remains to bear witness, as with Rembrandt's self-portraits at the end of his life. Drives and desires are no longer the raw nerve of existence but its residue. They lie at the bottom of a feeling of having lived. 'This was all that was left in the world: all the splendour and luxury, all the haunting obsessions, were

131 Ibid., p. 96.
132 Ibid., p. 242.
133 Genet, *Miracle of the Rose*, p. 173.

transformed into the quiet shivering of this coming and going.'[134] In writing on Rembrandt, Genet was anticipating Genet.

'My astonishment before a cornflower or a stone, the caress of a calloused hand, the millions of emotions that form me—I will disappear, but not them,' he continued in *Prisoner of Love*,

> Other men will perceive them, thanks to them, they will continue to be. I increasingly believe that I exist, along with other men, as the basis and proof that uninterrupted emotions alone run through creation. Another hand will know the joy of my hand in the hair of a boy, and already knows it, and if I die this joy will continue. 'I' can die—what has allowed this 'I' to be, what has made the joy of being possible, will continue the joy of being without me.[135]

Thus life, the whole of life, is suddenly contained within an instant and places its torch in the hands of the world . . . These admirable lines, as at peace as any could be at the coming of death, are all the more extraordinary in that they draw to a close—like a thread in fabric—the cycle of an existence founded on the 'refusal to continue the world'.[136] The point of this last work—this *finale*—is

134 Jean Genet, *Oeuvres complètes*, VOL. 5, *Le funambule*; *Le secret de Rembrandt* (Paris: Gallimard, 1979), p. 38 [our translation].

135 Genet, *Prisoner of Love* [our translation].

136 Genet, Letter to Jean-Paul Sartre, 1952 [our translation].

of course no more to 'continue the world' than any of the others before it but, rather, to imagine the world continuing from here, continuing without him. He had already had this experience of 'continuity', several times, but never with such calm, never so nakedly. Yes, once! Once, by way of a work which indeed liberated him, freed him from the world, holding only onto the 'extinguished flames', those little clumps of white and shadow where the feeling of being resides, 'that look at once soft and hard of *eternity passing*': the works of Alberto Giacometti. It was then that Genet first became a prisoner of love, writing out of admiration and love for the first time, without sexuality coming into it. Behind their ostensible differences, the two men shared a deep kinship, especially in terms of their mutual obsession: to free themselves from the illusions of space, to wrench life from the grip of reality, test it and hold on to it by way of a 'bygone age'. G the writer certainly had something in common with G the painter when he wrote: 'The faces painted by Giacometti seem to have accumulated so much life that they no longer have a second left to live, or a gesture to carry out, and (not that they [the faces] have died) they finally know death, because too much life has been crammed into them.'[137]

Giacometti also talks of this appearance which confuses life and death, in very similar terms:

137 Jean Genet, 'L'atelier d'Alberto Giacometti' in *Oeuvres complètes*, VOL. 5, p. 57 [our translation].

When, for the first time, I clearly saw the head that I was looking at fix itself, immobilize itself in the moment, definitively, I trembled with terror in a way I had never yet known and a cold sweat ran down my back. It was no longer a living head, but an object I was looking at as if it were any other object, no, differently, not like any other object, but like something that was simultaneously alive and dead. I gave a cry of terror as if I had crossed a threshold, as if I were stepping into a world never seen before. All the living were dead.[138]

It is not surprising that the creator of these solitary faces, freed from the weight of the earth and holding their heads in space, should have come back to haunt Genet as he wrote his final text. 'Each day, Alberto looked for the last time, he recorded the final image of the world,' he wrote in *Prisoner of Love*.[139] This was the same way he looked at the world of the Palestinian fighters which—absorbing his image—both kept him provisionally alive and brought him closer to death: 'I looked at the Resistance as if it were going to disappear the next day.'[140]

---

138 Alberto Giacometti, cited in Yves Bonnefoy, *Giacometti* (Paris: Flammarion, 1998), p. 290 [our translation].

139 Genet, *Prisoner of Love* [our translation].

140 Ibid. [our translation].

If Genet put aside his weapons and gave up on war in Alberto Giacometti's studio, if it was there that he found the air and the space to love without fear and to write about it fully and clearly, it was also because that air and space lightened the burden of the world, acting as a counter-weight to it. It was the place the enemy had no right to enter, where the father, defeated, no longer required defeating. 'With each one of his pictures, Giacometti leads us back to the moment of creation *ex nihilo*,' Sartre concluded in an article for *Temps Modernes*.[141] The image is entirely appropriate. What could be more liberating for Genet than this 'creation *ex nihilo*'? What could better suit his ceasefire than this utter abolition of all forms of ancestry, be they religious, social or familial? The same abolition which gave him the humility to write of Giacometti: 'I don't think he ever, not even once in his life, cast a con-temptuous glance on anyone or anything.'[142] The reader of *Our Lady of the Flowers* or *Funeral Rites* is unprepared, to say the least, to see these words from Genet's pen. How-ever, far from being an exception that proves the rule, this quote draws, down below the layers of make-up and the frills, from the centre, the depths of Genet, from the pri-vacy of an underground which he fiercely guarded from prying eyes. Because he did indeed have within him that

---

141 Jean-Paul Sartre, published in English as 'Giacometti in Search of Space' (Lionel Abel trans.), *Artnews* (September 1955): 26–9, 63–5.

142 Genet, 'The Studio of Alberto Giacometti', p. 324.

'great goodness' which he saw in Rembrandt and which he had to work at consistently taming, the way wild beasts are tamed, only showing its face to an *excepted* few, a *chosen* few. It was also as he wrote these pages on Giacometti that Genet first alluded to the well-known train journey where he felt a kind of 'shock . . . a kind of universal identity of all men'.[143]

It is no coincidence that this memory was taken up again and further developed a few years later in a second text on Rembrandt, published in 1967, *What Remains of a Rembrandt Torn into Four Equal Pieces and Flushed Down the Toilet* . . . In order for Jean Genet to give up attacking, defending and giving orders, the work of another had to serve as an outlet for his expression. It required a work that awed him and *looked at him* (the work of a painter or sculptor rather than of a writer). This was what was needed to free him from his dual role of actor and director, so that he could safely put aside his all-powerful 'I' and allow his dazzling intelligence to concentrate on the subject at hand.

Here is the account, set on board a train in 1953, of Genet's invisible and spectacular accident, his discovery of the common measure of all men. It was simultaneously the death knell for self-superiority and for his screen of narcissism:

143 Jean Genet, *What Remains of a Rembrandt Torn into Four Equal Pieces and Flushed Down the Toilet* (Bernard Frechtman and Randolph Hough trans) (New York: Hanuman Books, 1988), p. 12.

beauty. I quote at length, because it seemed impossible to cut the text further without mutilating its meaning.

Something which seemed to resemble decay was in the process of cankering my former view of the world. One day, while riding a train, I experienced a revelation: as I looked at the passenger sitting opposite me, I realized that every man has the same value as every other. I did not suspect (or rather, I did, I was obscurely aware of it, for suddenly a wave of sadness welled up within me and, more or less bearable, but substantial, remained with me) that this knowledge would entail such a methodical disintegration. Behind what was visible in this man, or further—further and at the same time miraculously and distressingly close . . . (graceless body and face, ugly in certain details, even vile, dirty moustache, which in itself would have been unimportant but which was also hard and stiff, with the hairs almost horizontal above the tiny mouth, a decayed mouth, gobs which he spat on the floor of the carriage that was already filthy with cigarette stubs, paper, bits of bread, in short, the filth of a third-class carriage in those days) . . . my gaze butted (not crossed, butted) that of the other passenger, or rather melted into it. The man had just raised his eyes from a newspaper and quite simply turned them, no doubt unintentionally, on mine, which in the same accidental way were looking into his. Did he then and there experience the same emotion—and confusion—as I? His gaze was not someone else's: it was my own that I was meeting in a mirror inadvertently and in a state of solitude and self-oblivion. I could only express as follows what I felt: I was flowing out of my body, through the eyes, into his at the same time as he was flowing into mine . . . what was it that had flowed out of my body—I had fl . . . and what had flowed out of his? . . . Was it because every man is identical with another?

Without ceasing to meditate during the journey, and in a kind of state of self-disgust, I very soon reached the conclusion that it was this identity which made it possible for every man to be loved neither more nor less than every other, and that it is possible for even the most loathsome appearance to be loved, that is, to be cared for and recognized—cherished. That was not all. My train of thought also led me to the following: this appearance, which I had first called vile was—the word is not too strong—was willed by the identity (this word recurred persistently, perhaps because I did not yet have a very rich vocabulary) which was forever circulating among all men and which a forlorn gaze accounted for. I even thought that this appearance was the temporary form of the identity of all men.[144]

Just as we imagine Rembrandt, in front of his mirror, dressed up to the nines, disguised as a merchant, as a biblical character and sometimes as a painter, with his berets, his crown-shaped hats, necklaces and earrings, his collars of lace or velvet or fur, and, beyond his arm buried under the cloth, his other arm and hand moving, bringing the scene onto the canvas, we must imagine Genet, the transvestite, casting his eye over his character's skilfully applied make-up, and with that same look, framed by a delicate mascaraed eye, bringing another to life, exposing him. This image, allowing for some blurring of the lines dividing the roles, gives us the duo that inspired Genet's work: theatre on the arm of solitude. The first acts as a mask for the second, the second as a prompter for the first. Genet concludes his text on Giacometti with these words: 'I am alone, the object seems to say, hence caught within a necessity against which you are powerless. If I am only what I am, I am indestructible. Being what I am, and unconditionally, my solitude knows yours.'[145]

Faced with Giacometti's works, as with those of Rembrandt, Genet's solitude no longer needs a theatre or

---

144 Ibid., pp. 10—17.

145 Genet, 'The Studio of Alberto Giacometti', p. 329.

a mask to speak itself. It has a double—a *doublure,* an understudy. 'Rembrandt,' he wrote, 'didn't really know how to capture the likeness of his models; in other words, he couldn't really see the difference between one man and another.'[146] Which makes for an unsettling parallel with the sculptor of *The Walking Man* (1961), who, in answer to the question 'Does it seem impossible to you to capture likeness?', replied, 'Likeness? I spend so much time looking at people I no longer recognize them.'[147] Thus we come full circle and are brought back to Genet's discovery that all people share a common identity. He sometimes interpreted this as something disgusting and sometimes, conversely, as an opening onto the 'quality' which for 'every man . . . seems to be a kind of ultimate recourse and owing to which he is, in a very secret, perhaps irreducible area, what every man is.'[148]

Several years later, Genet wrote *The Screens*, which marked the forcible entrance of 'ugliness' into his plays. The screen of beauty upon which his lyrical relationship with evil had been fashioned, acting as a backdrop for its masquerade of images, came apart. The meeting on the train, the discovery of the self in the other: '[the] identity which made it

---

146 Genet, *What Remains of a Rembrandt,* p. 60.

147 Alberto Giacometti, interview with Pierre Dumayet in *Écrits* (Paris: Hermann, 2008), p. 285 [our translation].

148 Genet, *What Remains of a Rembrandt,* p. 18.

possible for every man to be loved neither more nor less than every other, and that it is possible for even the most loathsome appearance to be loved, that is, to be cared for and recognized—cherished.'

All this, which had clouded and tarnished his counter-vision of the world, would clear itself a passage and find a name for itself with the 'family of nettles'. When he gave Leïla, Saïd's wife, the role of ugliness, the most horrifying ugliness, did Genet know in advance that he would put the finest outbursts of the play in the mouth of that 'ugly, stupid, thieving beggar'?[149] Saddled with all the defects the world could bestow, this hideous woman is not only the most endearing member of the family, she also embodies 'poetry', beauty turned back to front. And when it comes to giving orders—an undertaking very dear to Genet—it is again she, the one without weapons of her own, who commands with most force. Thus, to her angry husband, who tears a comb from her hands and orders her not to change her ugliness—'I don't want you to wipe your eyes or your dribble any more, I don't want you to blow your nose or wash yourself'—she responds:

> But I want—it's my ugliness, earned hour by hour, that speaks, or what speaks?—I want you to stop looking backward. I want you to lead me without flinching to the land of shadow and of

---

149 Jean Genet, *The Screens* (Bernard Frechtman trans.) (New York: Grove Press, 1962), pp. 108–9.

the monster. I want you to plunge into irrevocable grief. I want you—it's my ugliness, earned minute by minute, that speaks—to be without hope. I want you to choose evil and always evil. I want you to know only hatred and never love. I want—it's my ugliness, earned second by second, that speaks—you to refuse the brilliance of night, the softness of flint and the honey of thistles. I know where we're going, Saïd, and why we're going there. It's not just to go somewhere, but so that those who send us stay tranquil on a tranquil shore.

A long silence. Saïd takes off his shoe and empties out a stone which was bothering him. He puts it back on. He says quietly:

It wasn't you who set fire to the orange trees, was it?[150]

There is a great advantage to copying out a passage after reading it: the movements of the author, their choices, their progress, must be reproduced, word by word. In this case, as I followed Genet's movements, I could not stop picturing him, his back to the wall, bargaining with the past and present for another time, a time which both contains them and comes out of them. In the name of the past: 'I want you to choose evil and always evil.' In the name of the present: 'It's my ugliness, earned second by second,

---

that speaks.' In the name of another time: 'I want you to stop looking backward.' This is Genet's longest play, with the least clearly defined aims. This is surely because it represents a new and interminable quest: Where to go, when contradictions no longer dissolve before beauty, when beauty is no longer all-powerful?

Back to Rembrandt, or, rather, Genet, by way of the splendid portrait he made of the Dutch painter's later self-portraits.

> Agreeable to the eye or not, decrepitude is there. So it is beautiful. And full of . . . Have you ever had a wound, on your elbow, for example, which has become infected? . . . You must see, the whole organism goes to work *for* that wound. With every square centimetre of a metacarpus, or of Mrs Trip's lip, it's the same. Who achieved this? A painter who only wanted to render what is and who, painting it accurately, could not but give it all its force—and therefore its beauty? Or rather, a man who, having understood—after deep reflection?—that, as everything has dignity, he should endeavour to portray that which seemed to have none?

And a little after:

> Between himself and the world, maliciousness acts like a screen; it either makes him withdraw, breaks him down, or disguises him. Maliciousness,

and all other forms of aggressiveness, and all that we call character traits: our moods, our desires, eroticism and vanity. Slash the screen to see the world approaching![151]

In short, slash the screen of beauty. The very one Jacques Lacan would say is the last before death. 'The beauty effect is a blindness effect,' Lacan specifies. 'Something else is going on on the other side which cannot be observed.'[152]

In his final work, *Prisoner of Love*, Genet temporarily rebuilt the screen. He placed himself in the 'no world's land' of the fedayeen and cast his eye in two directions: acting as watchman during the day, on the lookout for the world's lying masks, and, as night-watchman, for the 'something else . . . on the other side'. It is this double stance that gave rise to his major divergences in tone. Transparency on one hand, manipulation on the other—with the Palestinians, as with theatre, when Genet lends his voice, he keeps hold of it—in short, the tension, the constant back-and-forth, between artifice and vision, hermeticism and confession. It is true that here, again, Genet pre-empts us, freely outing himself as a natural shammer, forewarning his reader: 'Once we see in the need to "translate" the obvious need to "betray", we shall see the temptation to betray

151 Genet, *What Remains of a Rembrandt*, p. 71.

152 Jacques Lacan, *The Seminar of Jacques Lacan*, BK 7, *The Ethics of Psychoanalysis, 1959–60* (Dennis Potter trans. and annot.) (Routledge: London, 1992), p. 252.

as something desirable, perhaps comparable to erotic exaltation'.[153] Or again, speaking of Abu Omar, the Palestinian
destined for arrest and death: 'I'm not sure I haven't made
him into a marionette, the sort of doll whose slack lips
showmen, and liars too, manipulate.'[154]

Nonetheless, when the time came to describe the 'motive'
for the journey—*Time Regained* in the form of a mother
and her son—Genet lost his abilities as a 'traitor', and for
good reason. He had always taken fantasy as the birthplace
of all fictional reality. For the first time he was moving in
the opposite direction. The way of the cross, one might
say. He would look for *proof* in reality of what may only
have been a fantasy: the feeling of having been, fourteen
years earlier, a temporary replacement for a Palestinian
fighter in the eyes of his mother, of having been her son
during Hamza's absence. In other words, of having known,
thanks to these two—with the father, of course, being
absent (we learn, incidentally, that he is dead)—what being
a son could mean.

The mother. In the *Prisoner of Love* there are phrases closed
tight like oysters. They must be read and reread in order
to gain access to their secrets. Those that deal with the
figure of the mother—most of the time based on the

153 Genet, *Prisoner of Love*, pp. 69–70.
154 Ibid., p. 352.

Virgin—almost all fall into this category. Almost all are elliptical. Some even push their elliptical nature so far that errors of syntax occur. It is true that Genet did not have all of his usual energy when editing the proofs, not long before his death. But, whether or not he intended it, one little slip escaped him. After having described Hamza's mother, 'a widow, but very strong; a mother armed exactly like her son, and in fact the head of the family', he follows, a few lines later, with 'remember the Black Virgin of Montserrat, showing her son as greater than herself, as taking precedence of her so that she might exist, and of the child so that he might live forever'. What meaning can we give to these words: 'the child so that he might live forever [*l'enfant, afin qu'il demeurât*]'? The structure of the sentence would indicate the following: '[but she] giving birth to him so that he might live [*l'enfantant afin qu'il demeurât*]'. Or, less probably, perhaps a verb is missing after *enfant*, but which verb? The next page gives us a clue. 'The fact that the Virgin Mary is called the Mother of God makes you wonder, since the chronological order is the same for parenthood human and divine, by what prodigy or by what mathematics the mother came after the Son but preceded her own Father.'[155]

In other words, God the father and God the son being one—at least in Genet's interpretation of Christianity—the mother comes after her son (God the Father) but

155 Ibid., pp. 191–2 [translation modified].

before her father (God as Christ). All in all, it is not so much the fact that a virgin could give birth to a son, which is the basis for Genet's irony, but the fact that the mother of the son could be the daughter of the father. This arrangement of roles, this fusion of the progenitor and the son fits his psychological equation. Better: it is the only one that plays his game.

However, as a final word, the meaning of 'child' in the amputated phrase must be sought 150 pages earlier. Recounting his discovery of the Virgin of Montserrat, Genet wrote: 'as the black Virgin proffered her child (as it might have been some hoodlum showing a black phallus), I sat down on a bench.'[156] However resistant one may be to psychoanalysis, in this case the extract leaves little room for doubt. This black Christ, brandished by his mother like a phallus, 'lives' in the place of the father, replaces him.

As God the father and the son were one, Genet could take on both roles. Father and son of his mother, who precedes and follows him, he *refashions* the Oedipus of Sophocles and Freud, that is, he reproduces it while switching the terms. What exactly happens to him in *Prisoner of Love* when he meets Hamza's mother for the first time? First there is the scene, during which 'the tall shadow' enters the darkness of the room and places a tray with a cup of

156 Ibid., p. 40.

Turkish coffee and a glass of water on the little end-table.
'Had she come out of the now ear-splitting darkness,' he
asks himself, 'or out of the icy night I carry about with me
everywhere?' A page later:

> Because he was fighting that night, I'd taken the
> son's place and perhaps played his part in his room
> and his bed. For one night and for the duration of
> one simple but oft-repeated act, a man older than
> she was herself became the mother's son. For
> 'before she was made, I was'. Though younger
> than I, during that familiar act she was my mother
> as well as Hamza's.[157]

In other words, Genet does not take the mother away
from the father—who has disappeared, been done away
with—he takes her away from the brother. Yet let us recall
the time he wrote: 'In the cell, I really and truly returned
to her throbbing breast and had real dialogues with her,
and perhaps these transformations which made Mettray
my mother added an incestuous feeling to my love for
Divers, who had come from the same womb as I.'[158]

Forty years later, this is how history follows on from
itself, transposes itself: 'Was the relationship between
Hamza and his mother peculiar to them, or were they both
obeying a general law among the Palestinians whereby a
widowed mother and a beloved son became one? By now

157 Ibid., pp. 192–3.
158 Genet, *Miracle of the Rose*, p. 196.

the couple, carried and nurtured inside me for so long, contained an almost incestuous element.'[159]

It goes without saying that this 'general law' is not found 'among the Palestinians' but originates in Genet's need, if he is to approach the figure of the mother, to be as far away as possible from the 'primitive scene' and its setting—France—as well as to be as close as possible to a symbolic, *unreal* situation, a *house of the living*, an 'enormous barracks' in the way prison had been. However, with the Palestinians in Jordan, Genet was not only outside of time and without territory, like in dreams, he was also a stone's throw away—though an impassable one—from the holy lands, from the place of Christ's birth and his execution.

In *Prisoner*, as in *Our Lady of the Flowers* and *Querelle*, transgression and 'incest' occur in the form of the same enclosed relation: two sons and a mother. One of the two sons, Genet in this case, alternatively inhabits each of the two states of the Christian God: omnipotence and crucifixion. This is, admittedly, remote from Jean, the cannibal in *Funeral Rites*, preparing to 'receive the totemic food', to eat Jean Decarnin.[160] Nonetheless, the desire for adoption, an adoption chosen by himself rather than willed by others, is still at work, searching, to the point of exhaustion, for a way out.

159 Genet, *Prisoner of Love*, p. 304.
160 Genet, *Funeral Rites*, p. 241.

I was sure that I was the god. I was God. Sitting alone at the wooden table, I waited for Jean, who was dead and naked, to bring me, on his out-stretched arms, his own corpse . . . I belonged to the tribe. And not in a superficial way by virtue merely of my being born into it, but by the grace of an adoption in which it was granted me to take part in the religious feast. Jean D.'s death thus gave me roots. I finally belong to the France that I cursed and so intensely desired. The beauty of sac-rifice for the homeland moves me.[161]

How could one not think here, faced with such a striking echo, of Freud's conclusions in *Totem and Taboo* (1913)? 'One day the expelled brothers joined forces, slew and ate the father, and thus put an end to the father horde . . . Now they accomplished their identification with him by devouring him and each acquired a part of his strength.'[162]

At the age of thirty-four, Genet made a totem in the form of an idealized brother and, setting him up as a god, 'absorbed' the father by eating the son 'knife and fork in hand'. As the end neared, this feast became merely the memory of a dead life. Genet had, solemnly, religiously 'absorbed' the father. All he had left to do was to put him-self back into the world before leaving it: to 'give birth' to

161 Ibid., p. 248.

162 Sigmund Freud, *Totem and Taboo: Resemblance between Psychic Lives of Savages and Neurotics* (A. A. Brill trans.) (New York: Dover, 1998), p. 122.

his mother. This would, inevitably, take the form of an apparition which is immediately followed by a merciless awakening. 'The mother', who, unlike the son, has no name, neither in *Prisoner of Love* nor *The Screens*, is destined for futility as soon as she comes into contact with reality. When Leïla Shahid asked him, not long before his departure, what compelled him to return to Jordan, Genet replied 'Shadow. I am looking for shadow.' He used the same word—shadow—to describe prison in his interviews with Antoine Bourseiller. And it was shadow again that had endeared Greece to him. 'For the first time,' he said, 'I saw something that for me was astonishing: shadows, yes, but mixed with light.'[163] And, again for the first time, he experienced the feeling of having a mother, when, lying on Hamza's bed, he heard two faint knocks on the wooden door and, as the door opened, saw her appear: 'The light from the starry sky entered the room, and behind it I could see a tall shadow.'[164]

Knowing that in order to make her—the mother—his, he needed to take her from a 'rival'—the brother—Genet's desire is all the more destined for failure as Hamza is absent when he finds her again. As absent as he could possibly be; he isn't merely out, he isn't away fighting, he is completely out of the country, in Germany. Suddenly, fourteen years later, in Irbid, a small village in Jordan, she whom he had

163 Genet, *The Declared Enemy*, p. 186.
164 Genet, *Prisoner of Love*, p. 192.

seen as 'a mountain' is not only old, toothless and almost bald, as decrepit as Rembrandt's Margaretha de Geer, she is also flat: 'as flat as Hussein's tin crowns stuck up over all the streets and squares; as the first fedayee crushed to death by a tank; as the empty uniform on the coffin of a dead soldier; as a poster; as a barley loaf; as a plate.'[165]

Flat, as you might say of a speech or a wine, flat and featureless, drab.

> Where could all the mother's coldness, dryness and mistrust have come from? From what dried-up stream? But metaphor didn't help. No image applied so well as the words 'dry' and 'dryness' themselves, connoting the absence of all that flows, that is liquid, that spreads out and irrigates. In those two words all is fixed and motionless, as in the mother . . . She'd been gay before, defending her cause with her gun and proud of her son. Now she was dried up.[166]

Hamza / His Mother. '[Their] relationship,' he wrote '[came] to live a life of its own inside me, independent as an extra organ or a developing fibroid.' Fibroid, even when benign, means tumour, and even though the word is given a positive value here, it cannot but relate back to the cancer at work in the body of the author. Who explains: 'It didn't worry me that this pair's destiny should continue with me

165 Ibid., p. 407.
166 Ibid., p. 414 [translation modified].

in this way, because their fate symbolized the resistance, at least as it had seemed to come to me in my thoughts.'[167]

Unlike the heel injury he deliberately allowed to fester—I mentioned it at the start of this book and he too mentions it in his story—Genet does not allude to his cancer in *Prisoner of Love*. Well, he does once, but, of course, without saying anything about it. It is difficult, however, not to see cancer, after close reading, as the 'undeclared' enemy—the enemy he could not anticipate, nor cast away from him, nor devour. An enemy over which his all-powerful will had no hold. Which is why I am tempted to say—if my simplification may be forgiven—that the Mother-Son fibroid was to his troubled morality, the death of his birth, what the wound in his heel was to his cancer: a place of resistance, a retaliation. Against hostile forces, the brutality of the Israeli state, the Americans and the Arab regimes, the Palestinian Resistance embodied the freedom, the audacity, the violence and the retaliation of the solitary man against the horde. Genet loved him, ingested him, incorporated him, made him his own in the most vital sense. In qualifying this 'Resistance' as maternal here, I am doing nothing more than paraphrasing him: 'The following digression will be quickly begun and quickly finished. The behaviour of some adult Palestinian men sometimes made me think of a maternal rather than a purely military attitude.'[168]

167 Ibid., p. 294.
168 Ibid.

The difference between the characters in his novels and plays and the fedayeen was that the fedayeen did not follow his orders. He said as much: 'The fedayeen didn't do as I told them, they didn't appear and disappear to suit my convenience. What I took for a long time to be a kind of limpidity, a total lack of eroticism, might have been due to the fact that each individual was completely autonomous.'[169]

These words, in associating eroticism with an absence of autonomy in the other, lead us to the very likely subordination of reality to fantasy in Genet's sexual life. It is also clear that behind the autonomy of each soldier hid the threat of power, of repression, of corruption. The very opposites of joy. However, Genet's love for the fedayeen never blunted his formidable critical powers. In fact, he needed them more than ever as the interference of the Authority threatened the very 'autonomy' of this mobile territory, this 'portable' country. Just after the 100th page of the book, the misgivings become clearer: 'I felt rather uncomfortable about the way the PLO were using the same devious and cynical methods . . . as ordinary states successfully established'.[170]

Further on, Genet spots danger among the fighters themselves: 'the deference, almost sycophancy, in the fedayeen's behaviour towards members of the Palestinian traditional or banking aristocracies'.[171] Or again, in the

169 Ibid., p. 205.
170 Ibid., p. 87.
171 Ibid., p. 103

most basic way: 'I found the manners of almost all the ordinary Palestinians, men and women, delightful. But their leaders were a pain in the neck.'[172] (The French construction employed in this last sentence—'autant me charmaient les manières de la presque totalité des hommes et des femmes du peuple palestinien, les responsables étaient emmerdants'—would normally require a repetition of the word *autant* before *les responsables*. Genet leaves it out, in a linguistic contortion typical of his last work). Then comes the somewhat visionary critique of an evil which few Palestinians would dare to attack head-on and which turned out to be, among other things, fatal for the credibility of the Palestinian Authority and its leaders:

> It took me several years to realize how some of the leaders—well-known ones whose names appear in Western newspapers—became dollar millionaires. It was tacitly known or half-known that the seas of the Resistance had thrown up not a few bits of flotsam and jetsam but a whole strong-box in which each of them had one or more drawers containing proofs of his fortune in Switzerland or elsewhere. Each knew what the others had, too, because their fortunes were often the result of a division of the spoils.[173]

172 Ibid., p. 280.
173 Ibid., p. 139.

As for his portrait of Yasser Arafat—a depiction rendered with skill and cunning—Genet begins gently, but only in order to better drive home the poisoned sting at the end:

> Was his lack of action thought, and so a continuation of action? That great spider, silently and imperceptibly spinning out his shimmering web as he drank coffee after coffee, gazing into the distance and letting me talk without listening to what I said—had he really got his eye on the other big spider, Golda Meir? He proffered a few words, wary as a fly picking its way over the web. Was that what he really was? Or was he playing the same game as Marshal Tlass in Syria?[174]

Steep and winding, like a mountain path, the passage shows another aspect of the style adopted by Genet in *Prisoner of Love*: from the main verb—'had he really got his eye'—to the object—'Golda Meir'—the words snake around, tack from side to side and feign retreat, secretly savouring in advance—not like a fly but like a scorpion— the blow they are preparing. The barrage of question marks indicates an encirclement strategy, rather than a sceptical attitude. Flanked by Golda Meir on one side and by Tlass on the other, Arafat is subjected to the most insulting comparison possible. Truth be told, if there is one writer who really expresses the full sense of the Latin expression *in cauda venenum*[175] it is Jean Genet. And when

174 Ibid., p. 141.

175 'The venom is in the tail.'

he goes for the head of the ridiculous Tlass, the wealthy Syrian defence minister who for thirty-two years divided his time between his army, his tacky 'poetry' and his flower collections—including a rose named after him—the heads of many Arab leaders fall with it into the guillotine's basket.

> 'To begin with, all the flowers in Syria, from the humble forget-me-not to the edelweiss, then strange blooms he called Assadia and Talarnia; then eighteen unattainable women: Caroline of Monaco, Lady Di, Miss World '83, Lady X, Louise Brooks, Lulu, etc., with a poem about each, published by his own publishing house.' That's what the Palestinians say about Marshal Tlass. One of the leaders told me, smiling, that despite the enormous rings he wears, he masturbates as he reads *Playboy*.[176]

'Genet is so constituted that his feelings have a double or triple bottom,' wrote Sartre.[177] Perhaps one might also say that Genet's feelings were so constituted that they performed double and triple changes of direction in order to attain their depths without dissolving. They sought, by any way possible, the means to overlay one another without erasing one another, to gainsay one another without unsaying one another. Clear-headedness and treason—

176 Ibid., pp. 141–2.
177 Sartre, *Saint Genet*, p. 527.

sometimes allies, sometimes at war—each arriving in their own time to sound passion's death knell. Hence the ambivalence, and therefore the accuracy, of the book's title: made a prisoner as much by himself as by the object of his love, the prisoner of love seeks, like all those in love, to remain a prisoner, and like all captives to escape. With this in mind, the following lines are eloquent:

> When I arrived, to an enthusiastic welcome from the fedayeen, I probably wasn't clear-headed enough to evaluate the opposing forces or make out the divisions within the Arab world. I ought to have seen sooner that aid to the Palestinians was an illusion. Whether it came from the Gulf or from North Africa it was ostentatious and declamatory, but flimsy. Gradually my feelings changed, especially after the 1973 war. I was still charmed, but I wasn't convinced; I was attracted but not blinded. I behaved like a prisoner of love.[178]

The Arabic language played a major role in keeping Genet prisoner of love. It fascinated him, but he knew very little of it.

In his final work, each time he sets out to discuss it or to translate it—to have it translated—he takes on the solemn tone of one who knows the secret of a world prohibited to mere onlookers, a world from which France is

178 Genet, *Prisoner of Love*, pp. 216–17.

excluded. The language and its unknown lands certainly contribute to the appeal of his last novel, to its 'peaks and troughs'. But on more than one occasion—particularly in dialogue—Genet's aims run up against it, like a rock. The distance he skilfully maintained between overheard dialogue and dialogues he composed, and recomposed, finds itself called into question, unbalanced, by a second kind of theatricality—more likely unintended this time—created by the fundamental incompatibility of Genet's daydream-translations and the Arabic language.

His errors in translation, in the strict sense of the term, also reveal to us something of his desire for that maternal language that was not his mother tongue, and which he could only catch glimpses of. To take just one example, there is the passage concerning the word Fatah.

> Fatah, then, or rather F.T.H., corresponds to the initials of the Falisteen (Palestine) Tharir (liberation) Haka (movement). In their French or logical order the three letters would give Haftha, which if it exists at all is meaningless. To get F.T.H. the order had to be reversed. Some overgrown children must have had a good laugh over that.[179]

For one thing, 'liberation' is not Tharir, but Tahrir, any more than 'movement' is not Haka but Haraka; for another, the three roots corresponding to the initials of 'Palestine Liberation Movement'—HArakat Tahrir

179 Ibid., p. 23 [translation modified].

Falisteen (HATF)—very much do have a meaning. HATF is one of the words signifying death in Arabic. This may be the reason the initials were inverted. Genet would doubtless have enjoyed learning that here, once again, death lurked behind the words.

Genet without doubt found Islam thornier than any other subject. He clearly stated his hostility towards all monotheistic religions, Islam included, on more than one occasion. He turned to paganism—to the respite of its cool shade—to disrupt the harsh and overpowering light of the one and only God. Greece, he told Bourseiller, was:

> The only country in the world where the people were able to venerate, to honour their gods and also not to give a damn about them. What the Greek people did in relation to Olympus, the Jews would never have dared and would still never dare to do for Yahweh, no Christian would dare to do for the Crucified, no Muslim for Allah. The Greeks were able at the same time to mock themselves and to mock their gods. That to me is astounding.[180]

On the other hand, Islam was not only a threat, from his point of view, it was also a victim, and additionally represented the most unified form of resistance against the West in general and Israel in particular. 'The state of Israel

---

180 Genet, *The Declared Enemy*, p. 187.

remains a "bruise", a contusion on the Muslim shoulder,' he wrote.[181] His choice of vocabulary—'Muslim shoulder' rather than 'Arab shoulder'—already contains, in itself, the contradiction he sought to resolve. It also reveals his intuition of the relative strengths of the Muslim and Arab identities, with the former, as could already be seen, gaining the upper hand. For though the Palestinian resistance was non-denominational and officially 'secular' in the 1970s and even into the 80s, Islamization was lying in wait during that shadowy time, when it became difficult to distinguish enemies from friends.[182] 'What I feared most,' he continued, 'were logical conclusions: for example, an invisible transformation of the fedayeen into Shiites or members of the Muslim Brotherhood.'[183] The clumsy use of 'Shiite', which doubtlessly corresponded in his mind with the 'Khomeinist Shiites', gives the sense of Genet's difficulty in attempting to think clearly on this subject (although he is not alone in that, to say the least). Further on, he again takes up the reins, pushing his argument further: 'it wasn't utterly out of the question that a fedayee might secretly harbour a potential Muslim Brother within himself' and, moreover, 'In the Middle East there was still a danger that a Palestinian might turn into a Brother, as a dog used to turn into a wolf. But as one of their leaders told me today,

181 Ibid., p. 73.

182 Literally, 'the grey hour "in which one can barely distinguish dog from wolf"' (Genet, *Prisoner of Love*, p. 67).

183 Ibid., pp. 254–5.

8 September 1984, that such a thing was impossible, let's pretend this digression was never either written or read.'[184]

In other words, we'll see who's right in the long run, once I'm dead. As has happened. The 'leader' was wrong, or else had patently sought to conceal the danger.

Genet approaches the subject in *Prisoner of Love* by starting with an article written by an obtuse Islamist. He clearly expresses his aversion—whoever the 'declared enemy' is— to blind and fanatic uses of religion.

> By page two I was completely stunned. The whole thing was full of hate. Things like: *We must fight everything that isn't Islam. For the time being we'll act through strikes . . . nothing is more offensive to man but pleasing to God than the fetid breath of a starving atheist or of a brother who's been on hunger strike for ten days.*[185]

All in all, the prisoner of love comes to the conclusion, during his narrative, that 'despite all the magical effects Islam, like Judaism, was a very opaque religion'.[186]

We will never know how Genet would have responded to the appearance of Osama bin Laden and his ilk on the world's political stage. But we do know, reading him

184 Ibid.

185 Ibid., p. 89.

186 Ibid., p. 363.

attentively, that he would have had serious problems tying the two strands together, that is to say, his hatred of America's politics on the one hand and religious fanaticism on the other. Asked by young Palestinian soldiers about the skyscrapers of New York, he replied: 'The skyscrapers in New York, with storeys of people in their intestines, emptied themselves violently, and then felt relieved, as after an attack of constipation. Until the eternal colic began again.'[187]

What other metaphor, following on the heels of this one, would he have dared to add in response to the destruction of the Twin Towers? Of course, we have no way of knowing. But behind this question without an answer is found—a reminder of how the seeds of hate are sown—the image he used to describe the destruction of the buildings of Beirut during the Israeli invasion.

> [It's amusing to sit] in Merkava tanks shooting at twenty-seven-storey blocks of flats; watching them double up like someone in fits of laughter; seeing that the cement, the steel girders, the balconies, the marble, all that had made the building's pride, were of the best possible quality. The block of flats turned into a white cloud slightly tinged with grey near the foundations, and shortsighted faces lit up.[188]

187 Ibid., p. 257.
188 Ibid., p. 350 [translation modified].

(He had already mentioned 'short-sighted faces' the page before. The 'Tsahal infantrymen . . . beardless short-sighted young philosophers with forget-me-not eyes, bifocal glasses and thin hairy arms sticking out of short-sleeved shirts' obviously got up his nose.[189])

For my part, I would like to point out a more or less forgotten fact, which is that it was not tank fire but Israeli cluster bombs which, in 1982, made a Beirut housing block full of hundreds of civilians collapse like a house of cards.

Two memories come to my mind in connection with the invasion.[190] One dates from the first days Lebanon was besieged by the Israeli army. I was working at Éditions du Seuil, where, apart from the director, Michel Chodkiewicz, very few of those around me were able to understand my feeling of horror at the events. Genet called me. 'How are you?' was all he asked. 'Bad,' I replied. The next day, to my great surprise, I saw him walk into the courtyard of 19 rue Jacob and, rather than heading straight for my desk, go through the main entrance, walk around the desks one by one, only stopping at mine after having made his presence known just about everywhere. 'Shall we go for a coffee?' I immediately asked him, certain that he had little interest in the comings and goings of journalists and authors. 'No,

---

189 Ibid., p. 348.

190 I should reiterate that I am not talking about the 2006 invasion, which started after I had written these words, but the 1982 invasion.

I'm staying here' was his reply, as he sat down across from me. I understood, after his departure, that he had come to protect me from solitude. Solitude again.

The second memory? An expression he used when we were in the company of a third person, though I cannot remember who. 'Do you know,' he had asked, 'what the difference is between Leïla and Dima?' He was talking about Leïla Shahid and myself. 'When lightning strikes Leïla, she shakes it off like crumbs from her apron. But when lightning strikes unexpectedly, Dima catches it in her apron.'

It is true that more than once I have had, the feeling of having caught lightning in my apron as I wrote this book. But now that I have done it, who knows? Perhaps I will find it easier to stop doing it now, or, more probably, find it easier to do again!

Genet travelled alone on the road to the Orient. Alone, in the most complete sense, in the sense meant by Nietzsche when, speaking of the 'recluse', he wrote 'in his strongest words, even in his cry itself, there sounds a new and more dangerous kind of silence, of concealment'.[191] In the end, he brought back an 'inaccessible' book, inaccessible like a grotto or monastery for which no path can be seen. You

191 Nietzsche, *Beyond Good and Evil*, n.p.

have to approach at night and advance patiently, feeling your way through the briars, to get close to the place.

> This book will never be translated into Arabic, nor will it be read by the French or any other Europeans. But since I'm writing it anyway . . . who is it for? . . . That elegant eighteenth-century edifice, the library of the harem in Istanbul, keeps its doors and windows shut. And the highest dignitaries of the countries that almost unwittingly made up the Ottoman Empire do their best to keep them shut.[192]

'If I say "darkness spread over all the world", I mean that at a certain moment everything seemed to coincide so closely with everything else that for a few seconds I experienced what might be called cosmic unity.'[193] In order to taste these 'few seconds', the author of *Prisoner of Love* simultaneously drew together both centuries and brief minutes. Weaving space and time into the same fabric, he worked at progressively removing himself away from any outside gaze, his own as well as his reader's. It was his final theatrical gesture, his last *calendar trick*, in defiance of what the 'West', he wrote, 'wants to do to the whole world'.[194]

---

192 Genet, *Prisoner of Love*, p. 289 [translation modified].

193 Ibid.

194 Jean Genet, 'L'Étrange mot D' in *Oeuvres complètes*, VOL. 4 (Paris: Gallimard, 1968), p. 10 [our translation]. 'Calendar trick' (*coup de calendrier*)

The aim of every event, be it intimate or public, should, in his eyes, contribute to 'bringing down the Christian era and the consequences of counting time from the moment of the Highly Contestable Nativity'.[195] Whether or not he intended to, the prisoner of love leaves us with the sense that his quest against historical, theological time was also his life and work's relentless retaliation against his own 'Highly Contestable Nativity'.

He thereby reaffirmed, up until his last second, his decision to be born, to live and to die outside of genealogy, without beginning or end, in the 'fresh and torrid shadow'[196] of a bygone age. Thus, he follows in the footsteps of his constant companions, Albrecht Dürer's *The Knight, Death and the Devil* (1513), from the engraving that Nietzsche and Giacometti held to be the greatest of works.

In fact his book was translated, in remarkable style, into Arabic.[197] It has also been read by more than one person in France or Europe, though by relatively few in comparison with the rest of his work.

Having asked him, one day, what he thought of a writer (whose name I forget), he responded with a crushing

---

is a reference from Jacques Derrida's famous text on Genet and Hegel: *Glas* (Lincoln: University of Nebraska Press, 1986). See p. 107.

195 Genet, *Oeuvres complètes*, VOL. 4, p. 10.

196 Ibid.

197 By Kadhim Jihad, Éditions Toubkal, Morocco.

epigram which I have never forgotten: 'A great writer is someone who writes very complicated things in a very simple way. A bad writer is someone who writes very simple things in a very complicated way.'

Perhaps it can be said of his last work that, dealing as always with complicated things, he would unhesitatingly proceed, if not in a complicated way, at least in a deliberately erudite, closed-off, hermetic way. And also, sometimes, in such a simple way that we end up asking ourselves if the locked door we had ran up against on the previous page even existed.

The essence of theatre is the need to create not merely signs but complete and compact images masking a reality that may consist in absence of being. The void.

Prisoner of Love, p. 83

The theatre will be placed as close as possible, in the truly protective shadow of the place where the dead are kept, or that of the lone monument which swallows them.

'L'Étrange mot D' . . .[198]

A work that was offered to the living of today and tomorrow but not to the dead would be what?

What Remains of a Rembrandt, p. 38

It is perhaps because death played dead in Genet's life that he ended up conceiving another death superior to it. A living death, gigantic, oceanic, ceaselessly stirred up and buoyed by new corpses. It was his pagan temple, the mass grave shared by all eras. His reservoir of night and

198 [Our translation.]

darkness. His mountain of shadow. On its slopes, he placed his life's work, his THEATRE. Not the theatre of his plays but his whole work. From there he waged, without limits, outside of time, with infallible cruelty and *délicatesse*, his war against order and law, against the fixed images of existence. Just as controlled fires are used to contain wildfires, Genet used death to contain the wildfire of appearances. In order to see, from under his masks, 'the white and deadly solitude' of life shine out.[199]

I now better understand why I wrote this book. Trying to understand Genet, following in his footsteps, led me to adopt the most appropriate position: placing oneself right at the heart of all contradictions, in the place where reality, weakened to the extreme, forces us to hold onto our vertigo in order to maintain our balance.

199 Genet, 'The Studio of Alberto Giacometti' [our translation].

ACKNOWLEDGEMENTS

Thank you to Albert Dichy for the sharpness of his observations and for the precious information he provided.

Thank you to Betül Tanbay, who enabled the end of this book to find its way.

BONNEFOY, Yves. *Giacometti*. Paris: Flammarion, 1998.

CHATEAUBRIAND, François-René de. *The Genius of Christianity; or, the Spirit and Beauty of the Christian Religion* (Charles I. White trans.). Baltimore, MD: John Murray, 1856.

———. *Memoirs from Beyond the Grave* (Robert Baldick trans., Philip Mansel introd.). London: Penguin Classics, 2014.

DERRIDA, Jacques. *Glas* (John P. Leavey, Jr. and Richard Rand trans). Lincoln: University of Nebraska Press, 1986.

DOSTOEVSKY, Fyodor. *The Brothers Karamazov* (Constance Garnett trans.). Calgary: Theophania, 2005.

———. *Crime and Punishment* (Constance Garnett trans.). Available at: http://goo.gl/WEGLF6; last accessed on 29 October 2015.

———. *Demons* (Richard Pevear and Larissa Volokhonsky trans). New York: Vintage Classics, 1994.

———. *Memoirs from the House of the Dead* (Jessie Coulson trans., Ronald Hingley ed. and introd.). Oxford: Oxford University Press, 1956.

FREUD, Sigmund. 'Dostoevsky and Parricide' (1928) in *The Standard Edition of the Complete Psychological Works of Sigmund Freud* (James Strachey trans., in collaboration with Anna Freud), VOL. 21. London: Hogarth Press / The Institute of Psycho-analysis, 1961, pp. 177–94.

——. *Moses and Monotheism* (Katherine Jones trans.). London: Hogarth Press / The Institute of Psycho-analysis, 1939. Available at: https://goo.gl/tsjmaV; last accessed on 31 October 2015.

——. *Totem and Taboo: Resemblance between Psychic Lives of Savages and Neurotics* (A. A. Brill trans.). New York: Dover, 1998.

GENET, Jean. *The Blacks: A Clown Show* (Bernard Frechtman trans.). New York: Grove Press, 1988.

——. *The Declared Enemy: Texts and Interviews* (Albert Dichy ed., Jeff Fort trans.). Stanford, CA: Stanford University Press, 2004.

——. *Funeral Rites* (Bernard Frechtman trans.). New York: Grove Press, 1994.

——. *L'enfant criminal* (The Criminal Child). Paris: Gallimard, 2013[1949].

——. *The Maids* (Bernard Frechtman trans.). London: Faber Finds, 2015.

——. *Miracle of the Rose* (Anthony Blond trans.). New York: Grove Press, 1988.

——. *Œuvres complètes*, VOL. 4. Paris : Gallimard, 1968.

——. *Œuvres complètes*, VOL. 5, *Le funambule; Le secret de Rembrandt*. Paris: Gallimard, 1979.

——. *Our Lady of the Flowers* (Bernard Frechtman trans.). New York: Grove Press, 1991.

——. *Prisoner of Love* (Barbara Bray trans.). New York: New York Review of Books Classics, 2003.

——. *Querelle of Brest* (Gregory Steatham trans.). London: Faber & Faber, 2000.

——. *The Screens* (Bernard Frechtman trans.). New York: Grove Press, 1962.

———. 'The Studio of Alberto Giacometti' in *Selected Writings* (Edmund White ed. and introd.). New York: Harper Perennial, 1995, pp. 309–39.

———. *The Thief's Journal* (Bernard Frechtman trans.). New York: Grove Press, 1987.

———. *What Remains of a Rembrandt Torn into Four Equal Pieces and Flushed Down the Toilet* (Bernard Frechtman and Randolph Hough trans). New York: Hanuman Books, 1988.

GIACOMETTI, Alberto. 'Entretien avec Pierre Dumayet' (Interview with Pierre Dumayet) in *Écrits*. Paris: Hermann, 2008, pp. 283–5.

LACAN, Jacques. *The Seminar of Jacques Lacan*, BK 7, *The Ethics of Psychoanalysis, 1959–60* (Dennis Potter trans. and annot.). Routledge: London, 1992.

NIETZSCHE, Friedrich. *The Antichrist* (H. L. Mencken trans.). New York: Alfred A. Knopf, 1918. Available at: http://goo.gl/UeLl1m; last accessed on 29 October 2015.

———. *Beyond Good and Evil* (Helen Zimmerman trans.). New York: Macmillan, 1914. Available at: https://goo.gl/PRg46; last accessed on 30 October 2015.

———. *Ecce Homo* (Anthony M. Ludovici trans.). New York: Macmillan, 1911. Available at: https://goo.gl/4U79KQ; last accessed on 29 October 2015.

———. *The Genealogy of Morals* (Horace B. Samuel trans.). New York: Boni and Liveright, 1910. Available at: https://goo.gl/Mke8xw; last accessed on 29 October 2015.

SARTRE, Jean-Paul. *Anti-Semite and Jew* (George J. Becker trans.). New York: Schocken Books, 1948.

———. *Saint Genet* (Bernard Frechtman trans.). Minneapolis: University of Minnesota Press, 2012.

WHITE, Edmund. *Genet: A Biography*. London: Vintage, 2004.

ALSO AVAILABLE FROM SEAGULL BOOKS

DOMINIQUE EDDÉ

Kite

Translated by Ros Schwartz

2012 | Cloth | 5" x 8" | 304 pages | $25

ISBN 978 0 8574 2 043 5

Rich and multilayered, with elements of both memoir and
fiction, *Kite* is at once a narrative of a passionate, and
ultimately tragic, relationship between Mali and Farid and
the simultaneous decline of Egyptian-Lebanese society.
Deftly evoking the intellectual scene of 1960s Beirut,
Lebanon's mountainscapes and the urban settings of Cairo,
Paris and London, this rich and evocative novel probes
memory with a curious mix of irony and melancholy,
ending in a place beyond hope and despair.

DOMINIQUE EDDÉ

Kamal Jann

Translated by Ros Schwartz

2014 | Cloth | 5" x 8" | 400 pages | $24

ISBN 978 0 8574 2 164 7

Dominique Eddé's gripping novel tells the story of the
doomed Jann family as they plot against one another for
revenge and power. Alliances, damaged lives, impossible loves
and deep betrayals unfold as the family relationships erode,
echoing the conflicts that tear apart the countries around
them. Expertly translated and rendered in a voice that is raw,
powerful and rich in imagery, *Kamal Jann* has been hailed by
critics as both universal and prophetic, a novel that is vital to
our understanding of Syria and the Middle East.

'A beautiful book, beautifully written with a pen dipped in line
accuracy, the accuracy of the look, the talent of the sketch,
without sacrificing the complexity of thought that underlies.'

Huffington Post

'Gripping . . . a novel of considerable power.'

World Literature Today